Basic Bible Sermons on the Cross

D1411556

BASIC BIBLE SERMONS

ON

THE CROSS

W. A. Criswell

BROADMAN PRESS
NASHVILLE, TENNESSEE

ISBN: 0-8054-2273-0
Dewey Decimal Classification: 232.963
Subject Heading: JESUS CHRIST — CRUCIFIXION — SERMONS
Library of Congress Catalog Card Number: 89-48573
Printed in the United States of America

Chapter 3 and Chapter 16 are taken from EXPOSITORY SERMONS ON GALA-
TIANS by W. A. Criswell. Copyright © 1973 by The Zondervan Corporation. Used
by permission.
Chapter 4 and Chapter 17 are taken from GREAT DOCTRINES OF THE BIBLE, VOL.
2 by W. A. Criswell. Copyright © 1982 by The Zondervan Corporation. Used by
permission.
Chapter 5 is taken from ISAIAH: AN EXPOSITION by W. A. Criswell. Copyright ©
1977 by The Zondervan Corporation. Used by permission.

Library of Congress Cataloging-in-Publication Data

Criswell, W. A. (Wallie A.), 1909-
  Basic Bible sermons on the cross / W. A. Criswell.
    p. cm.
  ISBN 0-8054-2273-0
  1. Jesus Christ—Crucifixion—Sermons. 2. Crosses—Sermons.
3. Atonement—Sermons. 4. Baptists—Sermons. 5. Sermons, American.
I. Title.
BT453.C75 1990
232.96 '3—dc20 —dc20   89-48573
                                                         CIP

Contents

1
The Shadow of the Cross

(John 19:16-18)

> Then delivered he him therefore unto them to be crucified. And
> they took Jesus, and led him away.
> And he bearing his cross went forth into a place called the place of a
> skull, which is called in the Hebrew Golgotha:
> Where they crucified him, and two other with him, on either side
> one, and Jesus in the midst (John 19:16-18).

There is a very famous painting of the Lord Jesus as a youth. He
looks to be in the picture something like eighteen years of age. He is
in the carpenter's shop, making yokes. Tradition has it that the easi-
est yokes to bear were those that were fashioned by the hands of our
Lord. In this picture as He stands working, in the way that He works
and in the way that He stands, over and beyond and behind Him
there is a shadow cast on the wall. It is the shadow of a cross. All the
days of the life of our Lord did He live in that shadow of suffering
and execution.

Jesus Living His Life
in the Shadow of the Cross

In Matthew 16:18 the Lord said to Simon Peter, ". . . Upon this
rock I will build my church;" Then we read in verses 21-23:

> From that time forth began Jesus to shew unto his disciples, how
> that he must go unto Jerusalem, and suffer many things of the elders
> and chief priests and scribes, and be killed, and be raised again the
> third day. Then Peter took him, and began to rebuke him, saying, Be it
> far from thee, Lord: this shall not be unto thee. But he turned, and
> said unto Peter, Get thee behind me, Satan: thou art an offence unto

me: for thou savourest not the things that be of God, but those that be of men.

Then in Matthew 17, after the glorious transfiguration, the Lord identifying John the Baptist as Elijah who had already come and to whom they had done whatsoever they listed, He says in verse 12: "Likewise shall also the Son of man suffer of them."
In Matthew 20:17 we read:

> And Jesus going up to Jerusalem took the twelve disciples apart in the way, and said unto them, Behold, we go up to Jerusalem; and the Son of man shall be betrayed unto the chief priests and unto the scribes, and they shall condemn him to death, And shall deliver him to the Gentiles to mock, and to scourge, and to crucify him: and the third day he shall rise again.

These passages in the center of the ministry of our Lord have I chosen, turning pages so few in number, to present how much the suffering death of Jesus was in His heart and before His face. He lived His life in the shadow of the cross. He was the Lamb slain from before the foundation of the world.

Great passages of the Old Testament, such as Psalm 22 and Isaiah 53, by prophecy depict the suffering of our Lord. When He was introduced to the world by John the Baptist, it was with the word, "Behold the Lamb of God, which taketh away the sin of the world." When He spoke to Nicodemus in John 3, Jesus said, "And as Moses lifted up the serpent in the wilderness, even so must the Son of man be lifted up." When He was anointed by Mary in the supper at Bethany, the Lord said, John 26:12 ". . . she did it (an anointing) for my burial." When the Greeks came to see Him from afar, He said, "Except a corn of wheat fall into the ground and die, it abideth alone. And I, if I be lifted up from the earth, will draw all men unto me. This spake He, signifying by what death He should glorify God." When He observed the Passover, He instituted the memorial of the Lord's Supper with these words, "This is my body broken for you; this is my blood of the New Covenant, shed for the remission of sins."

In Gethsemane He agonized before the cup that God had given

Him to drink. Finally the day of the cross came: cruel, harsh and awesome. Alone did He tread the winepress of the wrath and fierceness of Almighty God for our sins, and rich, red blood poured out.

> When Jesus came to Golgotha they hanged
>   Him on a tree.
> They drove great nails through hands and
>   feet and made a Calvary.
> They crowned Him with a crown of thorns;
>   red were His wounds and deep.
> For those were crude and cruel days and
>   human flesh was cheap.

The Shadow of the Cross
Over the World and Over Time

The shadow of that cross not only overshadowed the life of our Lord in all of His ministry, but the shadow of the cross has fallen across this world and the centuries of time. In the center of the world and in the heart of time our Lord has planted His cross, and the world can never be the same again because He lived here and died here. The scientists speak of worlds that are beyond and search to find if there might be life—other living creatures and maybe human races—on other planets and in other spheres. I do not think so, but however the discovery may be made, there will never be another plane or another sphere like this, because this is the world in which Christ died, and this is the earth that drank up His atoning blood. Nor can we ever be the same again because Christ lived and died and gave His life for us here.

Going through the heart of France one time, I stopped and walked through a British military cemetery. This was soon after World War II. As I walked through that cemetery, I stopped before the grave of a Royal Air Force pilot who had been shot down over France. Evidently his wife had come from England to visit the burial place of her husband. She had laid on the mound of earth a little bouquet of straw flowers and had written on the wreath these words: "Your wife and boys will never forget." What a wonderful and precious love! But how infinitely elevated when a like devotion is addressed to God! "We shall never forget." Out of all of the things in the life of our Lord, it was this that He asked for us to remember: "In remembrance of me."

Is it not a strange thing that beginning at the cross, the whole world flows out on either side? In the center of time, all the centuries before His day are B.C.—Before His cross. All of the centuries after His day are A.D.—In the year of our Lord. In the very heart of the earth and in the very center of time stands the cross of the Son of God.

In the shadow of that cross every Christian apostle, witness, martyr and preacher proclaimed the glory of our salvation found in His love and sobs and tears. In the shadow of the cross every apostle stood to preach. One of them declared, "God forbid that I should glory, save in the cross of our Lord Jesus Christ."

In the record of the New Testament they left behind, every word and every syllable is inspired by His suffering and stained by His blood.

The love and grace symbolized by the cross have blessed the hearts and homes and lives of the people for whom Jesus gave His life and poured out the crimson of His blood. What a marvelous and wonderful thing! The sin-sick soul, the despised and forgotten, those in sorrow and perplexity, those with insoluble problems to face and burdens that the heart can hardly bear—to them the message of the cross comes with hope and grace, heavenly remembrance and eternal salvation. It has become the very sign of our hope of heaven.

> If in Flander's fields the poppies grow,
> It will be between crosses, row on row.

Over the fallen form of those whom we have loved and lost for just awhile is a little cross raised high: a sign of our hope in God.

Before the Shadow of the Cross
We All Alike Are Welcome

The shadow of that cross, falling upon all mankind, has made us all equal and alike in Him. There are no big and no little; there are no wise and unwise; there are no poor and rich; there are no far off and favored nigh. But all of us are loved alike, cherished alike, accepted alike, saved alike, in the shadow of the cross.

In the Anglican church, as their habit of communion is, those who worship the Lord come forward and kneel to receive the elements of bread and the fruit of the vine. In a great cathedral in London there came forward the Iron Duke of Wellington. He was hero in British eyes. He was the man who delivered England and the continent from the ravages of Napoleon. England almost idolized the Iron Duke of Wellington. He came forward in the Anglican church and knelt at the altar to receive the bread and the cup. As he knelt there before the officiating Anglican minister, a ragged, wretched, poor man from the streets of London, unaware of the great Duke, came and knelt by his side. When the officiating minister saw it, he came to the outcast, touched him on the shoulder and said, "You must move away, for you are kneeling by the Iron Duke of Wellington." The great British commander, overhearing what the Anglican minister was saying, looked up and said: "Good sir, leave him alone. We are all the same before the cross." The ground is level at the cross. What a comfort that is to the poor and lost of the world! We are all alike loved of God.

The entrance before the majesty of God's glorious and eternal presence is open alike—not just to an officiating priest, not just to a presiding minister, not just to the great and mighty of the earth, but to the least and the smallest among us. When the Lord died and bowed His head and cried, "Father, into Thy hands I commend my spirit," there was a great shaking of the earth. The rocks were rent, the graves were opened, and the veil of the temple was torn in twain from the top to the bottom. Not from the bottom to the top as though a man's hands had done it, but from the top to the bottom, as though God had done it. The Holy of Holies was opened to view for the first time. The humblest man could see the sanctuary of God, and the basest man could walk into the very presence of the Lord God and call upon His name. What a marvelous thing God in Christ hath done for us! We all are welcome.

As the eloquent author of the book of Hebrews says in Hebrews 12:18-24:

For ye are not come unto the mount that might be touched, and that burned with fire, nor unto blackness, and darkness, and tempest, And the sound of a trumpet, and the voice of words; which voice they that heard entreated that the word should not be spoken to them any more: (For they could not endure that which was commanded, And if so much as a beast touched the mountain, it shall be stoned, or thrust through with a dart: And so terrible was the sight, that Moses said, I exceedingly fear and quake:) But ye are come unto Mount Sion, and unto the city of the living God, the heavenly Jerusalem, and to an innumerable company of angels, To the general assembly and church of the firstborn, which are written in heaven, and to God the Judge of all, and to the spirits of just men made perfect, And to Jesus the mediator of the new covenant, and to the blood of sprinkling, that speaketh better things than that of Abel.

Come, kneel and pray and lay before Him all of the problems and burdens of life.

> I heard the voice of Jesus say,
>   "Come unto Me and rest:
> Lay down, thou weary one, lay down
>   Thy head upon my breast."
> I came to Jesus as I was,
>   Weary and worn and sad.
> I found in Him a resting place,
>   And He has made me glad.

2
What Shall I Do with Jesus?

(Matt. 27:22)

Pilate saith unto them, What shall I do then with Jesus which is called Christ? They all say unto him, Let him be crucified (Matt. 27:22).

"What shall I do then with Jesus which is called Christ," the cry of Pontius Pilate, the Roman procurator who was faced with the decision concerning what to do with Jesus, is the ultimate cry of us all.

There are in the pages of the Bible some tremendous questions. Cain asked, "Am I my brother's keeper?" Moses asked: "Who is on the Lord's side? Let him come and stand by me." Job cried, "If a man die, shall he live again?" David asked, "What is man that thou are mindful of him, or the Son of Man, that thou visitest him?" Malachi asked, "Will a man rob God?" The Philippian jailer asked, "What must I do to be saved?" Hebrews 2:3 asks, "How shall we escape, if we neglect so great salvation?" The cry in the Revelation is, "For the great day of His wrath is come and who shall be able to stand?" But out of all the questions that are raised in the Bible, there is none more pertinent for us than the cry of Pontius Pilate, faced with a decision that he could not escape, "What shall I do then with Jesus which is called Christ?"

"Never man spake like that man." He said, "He that believeth on me is not condemned, but he that believeth not is condemned already because he hath not believed in the name of the only begotten Son of God." He further said, "He that believeth on the Son hath everlasting life: and he that believeth not the Son shall not see life;

but the wrath of God abideth upon him." He also said, "Except ye repent, ye shall all likewise perish." What shall we do with His words?

What shall we do with His life? Was there ever a life, reaching out toward us like the life of our Lord? He said, "The Son of Man is come to seek and to save that which was lost." I am lost in sin, facing inevitable death. His hands in mercy and grace reach out toward me. What shall I do with His life?

What shall I do with His death—an atoning death for me? The Roman centurion who presided over His execution said, "Truly this was the Son of God." Our Lord said, "This is my blood of the new covenant shed for the remission of sins." What shall I do with His death?

What shall I do with His glorified, resurrected, transfigured life? He that was dead is now alive forever more and He has the keys of hell and of death. Thomas said, "Except I see . . . in His hands the print of the nails, and put my finger into the print of the nails, and . . . thrust my hand into His side, I will not believe." Jesus appeared suddenly and turning to Thomas said, "Reach hither thy finger, and behold my hands; and reach hither thy hand, and thrust it into my side: and be not faithless, but believing." And Thomas answered and said unto him, "My Lord and my God." What shall I do with His resurrected and glorified life?

There are five evasions of Pilate when he faced that inevitable and destiny-determining question of "What shall I do then with Jesus which is called Christ?"

(1) He reasoned about it. "I find in Him no fault at all," Pilate said. They replied, "Were He not a malefactor, we would not have brought Him unto thee." Pilate said, "You take Him and you judge Him and try Him according to your law." They said, "By our law He should die, but capital punishment is not in our hands, therefore we have brought Him to thee." Pilate, having scourged Him and the soldiers having buffeted Him and mistreated Him and spat upon Him and plucked out His beard, brought Him forth and seeking to excite the pity of that infuriated mob said, "Behold the man." They

cried out the more: "Crucify Him, crucify Him. Away with Him." When you reason with Satan, you have a lost cause. There is no man yet ever able intellectually or emotionally, in his own ableness, to reason with Satan. The Adversary will win every time.

(2) Pilate sought to turn Him over to someone else. Let others make the decision for me. I shall do what they do. Having heard that He was from Galilee, under the jurisdiction of Herod Antipas, He was sent to Herod. Herod thought that a miracle worker would entertain him for an idle moment, but in disgust, Herod sent Him back to Pilate. Jesus was still on Pilate's hands.

There are some places and some times in our lives when we stand alone and naked before God, and this is one of them—when we decide for or against Christ. There are times when a man should take into his counsel all who are concerned—his business, family, destiny. There are times when a man should take into his confidence just his family. There are times when a man should discuss the problem he faces with just his wife. But there are times when a man has to face a question alone and decide it by himself, and this is one. Some day I shall die for myself. No man can die for me. Some day I shall be judged for myself. No man can be judged for me. The decision I make about Christ is deeply and everlastingly single and purposeful. "What shall I do then with Jesus?"

(3) Pilate sought to compromise. He tried to scourge Jesus and let Him go. How many times do we find that, when a man wrestles about giving his heart to Jesus, he compromises the decision. We try to give up drinking or cursing or shady deals, anything except yield our hearts to Christ. We try just to live a better life—compromising that inevitable question, "What shall I do then with Jesus?" But the question comes back, however I compromise it. I may give up a thousand evils and may reform every other day and resolve to live a perfect life from this moment onward, but the question repeatedly is pressed on my heart. I have not yet dealt with Him.

(4) Pilate attempted to substitute somebody else. He sought to substitute Barabbas, to leave Jesus alone. That attempted substitution pressed the question so earnestly to his heart. They chose

Barabbas. Pilate, in desperation cried, "What shall I do then with Jesus which is called Christ?"

So often a commonality in life is this attempt to substitute something else for the faith that saves and the Christ that can deliver. Always the ensuing result is tragic and sorrowful in the extreme. There is one name by which we are saved. There is one way by which a man can enter the gates of glory. There is only one life that God has poured out into the earth for us and that is the saving life of Jesus Christ.

In one of my little country churches there was a farmer—a chain smoker—who developed a sore on his lip. It was diagnosed as cancer. He was advised by the doctor to go to a larger city and have that cancer removed. He had a farmer friend and neighbor who was cultivating the land next to him. The friend said: "Why take all the time and travel and money to go to this doctor in the city and to the hospital to have that sore treated? I have a little vial of medicine at home that will heal it for you and it will save you all that trouble." So the neighbor brought him the vial of medicine and he put the medicine on the sore. The days and months passed and when finally he came to the surgeon, it was too late. He died with a cancer that had literally eaten away his face. Substitutes may be well in some areas, but they are not permissible when a man faces life and death. How little else is a man able to accept a substitute when he faces the judgment and eternity! Our souls are in the balance.

(5) Pilate's last attempt at compromise was no less fatal. "Pilate took water, and washed his hands before the multitude, saying, I am innocent of the blood of this just person: see ye to it." But he delivered Jesus to execution just the same. Jesus died under the execution mandate of the Roman procurator whose name was Pontius Pilate.

I was in Lucerne, Switzerland, some years ago. The mountain before the city is called Mount Pilate. I thought how unusual a thing that it would be called that. A friend said, "It is named after Pilate, the Roman procurator." Then I remembered that Pilate fell into Caesar's disfavor and was recalled. When he committed suicide they threw his body into that lake. Those peasants to this day say that in the midst of the early morning they have seen the body of Pontius

Pilate rise from the depths of the lake and wash his hands in the clear, blue water. A man cannot wash his hands of Christ. A man cannot wash his hands in death. A man cannot wash his hands of the judgment. A man cannot wash his hands of God. It is an inevitable question that every soul shall face for himself, "What shall I do then with Jesus which is called Christ?"

3
The Offense of the Cross

(Gal. 5:11)

And I, brethren, if I yet preach circumcision, why do I yet suffer persecution? then is the offence of the cross ceased (Gal. 5:11).

In Galatians 5:11 we find these words, ". . . then is the offence of the cross ceased." The Greek word in the text for "offence" is *scandalon*. "Then is the *scandalon* (and the English word 'scandal' comes from it) of the cross ceased." We have met that word before in 1 Corinthians 1:22 ff, where Paul wrote: "For the Jews require a sign, and the Greeks seek after wisdom: But we preach Christ crucified, unto the Jews a stumblingblock, and unto the Greeks foolishness; But unto them which are called, both Jews and Greeks, Christ the power of God, and the wisdom of God." In that text is the word, "offence." "The Jews require a sign, and the Greeks seek after wisdom: But we preach Christ crucified, unto the Jews a *scandalon*, 'offence,' here translated 'stumblingblock.'" The Gospel message to the Jews was a *scandalon*. To the Greeks it was *morion*, "idiocy," "foolishness," "moronic." But unto us who are saved it is Christ the "dunamis," the "power" of God.

That word, the *scandalon* of the cross, the offense of the cross, aptly described the attitude of the enemies of the Christian faith toward the cross of Christ. The Judaizers against whom Paul is addressing this letter to the churches in Galatia were most content to name and to accept Jesus as a great man, a good man. His words of mercy, His deeds of forgiveness, His kindness, His compassion, all were beautifully acceptable, but as a way of salvation His cross was a *scandalon*. It was an offense, it violated the properties of life. For a man to be saved by rituals, ceremonies, obediences to commandments and the keeping of laws was perfectly reasonable and natural and one that they promulgated, but that a man could be saved by trusting the Christ of the cross was a *scandalon*. The offensiveness of the execution of Christ!

The Cross as It Is Accepted Today

This letter to Galatia represents a day of nineteen hundred years ago. Is the cross a *scandalon*, an offense today? How things have changed! The cross today is looked upon as a part of the culture of western civilization. In many instances men build churches on the plan of the cross: there is the nave, the trancepts, and the central altar in the apse. The cross is placed high on the top of our tallest steeples as the sign and the aegis under which we are proud to march. The cross is embossed on our Bibles. It is a piece of jewelry, worn as an ornament around our necks. It is used in the ecclesiastical decoration of all the churches of Christendom. It is an object of art. Even the poet who may not at all have any conversance with the faith will use the cross as an acceptable image in his poetic lines. The whole world has come to accept the cross as a sentimental sign of dedication and self-sacrifice.

Is the cross offensive today? Actually, this day is no different than the day of the Apostle Paul. The same offensiveness, the same *scandalon,* that was found in the cross in the day of the apostles is no less true in our day and in our generation. It was with keen insight that Isaiah said "He hath no form nor comeliness, and when we shall see him, there is no beauty that we should desire him" (Isa. 53:2b). In that same vein Paul wrote these words, "For the preaching of Christ crucified is to the Jew an offence and to the Greek it is moronic idiocy" (cf. 1 Cor. 1:23). Today, as in that day, the beautiful life of Jesus is as perfume. To follow the Lord around the shores of Galilee, to look upon the Christ of the Sermon of the Mount or the Christ of the golden rule or the Christ of the compassionate, forgiving Savior, or the Christ of superlative pedagogical wisdom is acceptable. But actually the Christ of the cross is as scandalous, as offensive, today as it was then.

Interesting to me was a story that happened in the days of Thomas

Carlyle. He was in London and the guest of a glittering socialite. She was light of mind, one of those butterflies that lives on the surface, sipping here, sipping there. In the course of the conversation she began to speak of the guilt of the Jewish people in slaying the Son of God, the Savior of the world. She said that if Christ were to come today we would open our homes to Him and welcome Him. Then she said to Mr. Carlyle, "Do you not agree?" The great Scot essayist replied (and I copied down his answer): "No, I do not agree, madame. I think that had He come very fashionably dressed with plenty of money and preaching doctrines most palatable to the higher orders, I might have had the honor of receiving a card from you on the back of which would be written 'to meet our Saviour.' But if He came uttering His sublime precepts and denouncing the Pharisees and associating with publicans as He did, you would have treated Him much as the Jews did and cried out, 'Take Him to Newgate and hang Him!'" It is quite problematical whether if the Lord came today that He would be any more generously received or more devoutly believed in, accepted, than He was in the days of the Apostle Paul, for the offense of the cross, the *scandalon* of the cross, is not ceased.

How can such a thing be said in the cultured society in which we live and in the manifest degree of civilization into which we have advanced? There are three answers that explain why the cross is a *scandalon*, an offence, today, yesterday, in the generation that is yet to come, and throughout the centuries of human story.

The Cross as an Exposition of the True Nature and Character of the World

Reason number one, the cross is an offense because it exposes the real nature and heart of the world. Cheap sentimentality deifies humanity and glosses over the iniquity and the wickedness in the human heart. The cross opens our real nature to public view.

It was interesting to me to read about a famous church in Edinburgh in which one minister preached at the morning hour and another minister preached at the evening hour, both of them fellow pastors of the church. The man who stood up at the morning hour said that there is an inherent veneration for goodness in the heart of man. If virtue and goodness were to appear it would immediately be enthroned and received in adoration on the part of all mankind. At the evening hour his fellow minister, apparently unaware of what the other one had said in the morning hour, said, "Moral goodness and beauty of life and character came incarnate into this world and instead of being enthroned, humanity took Him, mocked Him, ridiculed Him, finally nailed Him to a cross, and He died in shame on a tree." Which one of those two ministers was correct? History says it was the second minister who really portrayed the depth of the depravity of the human heart. All we need to do is to read the pages of history and especially the pages of the Bible to confirm that judgment upon the human race.

In Genesis 6 it says, "And God saw that the wickedness of man was great in the earth, and that every imagination of the thoughts of his heart was only evil continually" (v. 5). And the rest of the story verifies that judgment from heaven. The story of Israel and the story of Judah is one of constant relapse into sin. The story of Nineveh and the story of Babylon is one of ruthless, merciless cruelty. The story of the whole human race is summarized in the first chapter of the Book of Romans. I do not read it in public; I never heard of anyone reading it in public. Yet it is a characterization of the Roman Empire and Roman civilization. It sounds like a description of the morality in America today. But as terrific an indictment of the human race as we find in the pages of secular history, there is no exposing such as we find in the crucifixion and the cross of the Son of God. John 20 says that He was hanged, He was nailed to the tree outside the city wall, outside the city gate on the main highway that leads into Jerusalem. The multitudes passed by. They saw the pain and they heard the crying and the sobs of the Son of God. Yet they looked upon His tears in silent indifference.

That cross is a rebuke to the entire human race. It is a rebuke to Herod Antipas with his coarse vices and his cheap revelry; to Caiphas, the scheming high priest; to Pontius Pilate, the Roman governor with his eye on his career and his place; to Judas Iscariot with his covetous, traitorous deeds; to the Roman soldiers, gambling at the foot of the cross for His fifth garment; to the Pharisees, the Scribes, the leaders of the religion of the nation as they mocked Him; to the throngs as they sat down in indifference or passed by in silent unconcern; even to the disciples themselves as they forsook Him and fled; and to Simon Peter as he denied three times that he ever knew Him. Like the shadow of the wings of the death angel that passed over Egypt in the night of the Passover, the shadow of depravity covers the whole human race. The crucifixion of Christ was a judgment upon the city, upon the state, upon the empire, and upon all humanity. And we are no different! The sin and the violence of which mankind is capable is without measure.

The Cross as a Call to Self-Denial and Repudiation of the Rewards of the World

Reason number two, the offense of the cross, the *scandalon* of the cross is no less so today because it is a call to self-denial and a repudiation of the rewards of the world. One can see that pointedly in the life of the rich young ruler. He was noble in every respect. He had kept the commandments, he told the Lord, from the days of his youth, from his youth up. And the Lord looking upon him loved him. He was the epitome of worldly success. The rewards and the emoluments of the social order had been heaped upon him. He was rich, he was young, and he was a ruler. When he asked the Lord concerning the eternal life preached by the prophet of Galilee, the Lord said to him: "There is not room enough, the way is not wide enough, for a man to go into heaven with his heart bound up in what he possesses. Get rid of the excess baggage. Give it away. It is trash. It is nothing. Get rid of it." And the next sentence says, "Come, take up your cross and follow Me." The Scriptures say that the lad was sad at that saying and went away grieved, for he had great possessions. Ah, how different does Christ look at things and does Christ look at the world in contrast to how the world looks at itself. In the last chapter of Paul's last letter he said, "Demas hath forsaken me, having loved this present world" (2 Tim. 4:10).

Oh, I grant you it is romantically interesting to follow in the steps of the Teacher along the blue shores of the Galilee. It would be most interesting to join the parade of Palm Sunday and enter into the City of Peace, into Jerusalem, in the day of the triumph of our Lord. But to take His cross and to go outside of the city bearing His reproach is a *scandalon* and an offense. It is something different.

For example, who wants to be a prude? And who wants to be a square? Who wants to be looked upon as Puritanical and Victorian? We have the desire to be set forth and to be accepted, and, if one is young enough, to be popular. I sat at a civic meeting here in Dallas. Strange thing to me, it was supposed to be a religious meeting, one of these affairs that Dallas presents as pulling all of the community together back of a common philanthropy. Well, I was seated in a big ballroom between two laymen. I was the pivot man in between. On one side and on the other side they talked about their drinking, their gambling, their promiscuous whoremongering, back and forth. And I, a minister, was expected to be a good sport. Why should I think anything of their gambling? Why should I say anything about their drinking? Why should I think anything of their whoremongering? After all, we all are to be good sports. Who wants to be prudish or square or Puritanical or Victorian? At the end of the meal I said to the men, "Before I leave I would just like for you to know that my heart is not in sympathy with anything that you men have discussed and joked about at this dinner meeting today."

The politician wants to be known as a good sport. He does not want to be a square, Puritanical, or prudish. What would the brewery, the distillery, the pimp, the gambler, and the bookie say about a puritanical politician? The liquid pot industry is infiltrating into every legislative hall in the land. The politician in order to be a good sport says "damn" and "hell" and he drinks and he gambles a little. That is what it is to be accepted by the world. The *scandalon*, the offense of the cross is overwhelming!

Take anything that the world prizes. Name it. Look upon the man who is acceptable in our culture and in our society. What kind of a man is he? He is a man of success. He is affluent. He has all of the accouterments of wealth. As such he is to be respected and admired. Those are the standards of the world. The Lord is so different! What the world had to offer was nothing to Him. And the followers of

Jesus who most sincerely live in the Spirit of our Lord are those who have that same persuasion in their hearts concerning the blandishments, the rewards, the stipends, the accumulations, and the embellishments of the world. In themselves accumulations are nothing, nothing at all. They do not even weigh in the balance.

There was a shabbily dressed man who lived on his small salary in a little house. He was known as being stingy, penurious, and frugal. The pastor ate dinner, a sparse meal, with that shabbily dressed man in his humble little cottage. The pastor was astonished to learn that that humble man had taken his salary and had tried to live on as small a part of it as he could, and with the rest of his salary he had supported a missionary on the foreign field. Was this man a worldly success? Who would want to emulate his poverty? Look at his dress! Look at his success! Look at the house that he lives in! Look at him! Who would follow that? Truly, there is such a difference between how God sees a thing and how the world regards it. Why, I can remember a deacon of many years ago who had served in my church for a generation. He came to church on a bicycle. In his old age a car struck and killed him while he was riding his bicycle. I buried him. He gave every penny he possessed to the church. I am not saying that one ought to do that nor am I implying that to be a true follower of Christ we must give all our living to the work of our Lord. The Lord never told Zacchaeus to sell everything he had. The Lord did not say that to Nicodemus or to Joseph of Arimathaea, both of whom were wealthy men. I am merely pointing out that in our sight, in our judgment, sometimes what we think is tremendous success in God's sight is a peccadillo. It is inconsequential or insignificant. Some things that we regard as so despised and rejected may be in God's sight prized beyond measure. The *scandalon* of the cross is a call to self-denial and a repudiation of the cheap rewards of the world.

The Cross as the Only Way of Salvation

Third, why the offense of the cross, the *scandalon* of the cross? Because it is presented in the Bible, in the Word of God, in the preaching of the Gospel of Christ as the *only* way of salvation. It is presented thus openly, pointedly, vehemently, vigorously. There is no doubt of the clarity of the message of the Word of God regarding the way to be saved. It is *the* truth, it is *the* way, it is *the* life, and there is none other. It is as Simon Peter stood up and proclaimed, "Neither is there salvation in any other: for there is none other name under heaven given among men, whereby we must be saved" (Acts 4:12). Oh, when the Gospel message is presented as the Bible and the Holy Scriptures present it, it is always that. It is not Christ possibly. It is not Christ alternatively. It is not Christ among many others. It is the Lord Christ alone and that is an offense, and a *scandalon* to most of the world.

Why is the world offended at the way of salvation? There is only a small minority in the world that does not believe that there are many ways to heaven. They say we are all striving to get to the same place. The Buddhist goes his way, the Mohammedan goes his way, the Shintoist goes his way, the Confucianist goes his way, the Taoist goes his way, and all of the other faiths go their way, and among them the Christian goes his way. We are all striving for the same thing and going to the same place. They say that if a man is sincere in his Judaism, or sincere in his Islamic faith, or in the veneration of his ancestors, as is a good Confucianist, or whatever he is, he is just as certain of heaven and as certain to be saved as the Christian who looks in faith to the blood of Christ. This attitude is almost universally accepted. When the Christian, therefore, stands up and says there is no other way to heaven and there is no other message by which we can be saved than the cross of Jesus Christ, his faith becomes a *scandalon* and an offense.

Even the liberal ministers deny the effect, the cleansing, the atoning power of the blood of Christ. Such a bloody way of salvation is unthinkable to their sensitive souls. They refer to it as a "butcher's block" religion and a "religion of the shambles." I have been in churches where all of the hymn books were purged of songs on the blood. To the liberal minister Christ is a good man. He is a heroic man. He is an ideal man. But He is not in any wise looked upon in this liberal world as being the Savior who cleanses up through His blood. That is an offense to modern culture and society.

It has always been interesting to me how the Christian faith is uncompromising in its proclamation that the way of salvation is *Christ* and nothing else! There is no alternative. It is Christ or it is nothing. Believing in Him we are saved. Refusing Him we are lost.

The Roman Empire was the most tolerant, the most liberal, the most wise, and the most accurate in its handling of the many provinces and religions of its empire of any kingdom that ever existed. Men could worship, have temples, and do as they pleased. And yet the Roman Empire and the Caesars persecuted the Christians. Why? For one simple reason: the Christian refused to compromise his faith with any other religion whatsoever. When the Romans invited them to place Jesus in their Pantheon beside Jupiter, by the side of Juno, by the side of Neptune, by the side of Isis, by the side of Osiris, the Christian flatly refused. It is Christ alone. When the Christians were invited just to bow down before the Roman image, their lives could be spared if they would merely take a pinch of incense and put it on the fire that burned in the presence of the image of the Roman Caesar. The Christian died rather than compromise with a pinch of incense. I am telling you what is the faith of the New Testament, the faith of the martyrs, and the faith of the true men of God through the centuries. That kind of a faith is uncompromising. There is no salvation in any other.

The depraved heart of humanity does not change. We may have learned in some instances to be a little astute in how we address our violence. Years ago it may have been with an ax, a stone, or a club. It may have been with an arrow and a spear or with a musket and a rifle. Men are more sophisticated today. We do the same violence with a jet bomber or with dynamite or with hell-bombs. But the depravity of the human heart is just the same. The offense of the cross and the *scandalon* of the message of Christ ultimately is no more acceptable today than it was in the generations that have passed. Nor will it be more acceptable in the generations that are yet to come, until the Lord returns from heaven and brings righteousness to the war-weary, sin-cursed earth.

Dear God, help us through these unfolding years. Master, let there be less and less of us and more and more of Thee until there be none of us and all of Thee. Lord, help us in our judgment to see things as they really are. Help us not to be blinded by the tinsel, tinfoil, and the cheap glitter of the world, but to see things as those who endure, looking upon the invisible. Grant it, God, please.

4
Our Lord's Entrance into Suffering

(Heb. 2:9-10,14-15)

But we see Jesus, who was made a little lower than the angels for the suffering of death, crowned with glory and honor; that he by the grace of God should taste death for every man.

For it became him, for whom are all things, and by whom are all things, in bringing many sons unto glory, to make the captain of their salvation perfect through sufferings.

Forasmuch then as the children are partakers of flesh and blood, he also himself likewise took part of the same; that through death he might destroy him that had the power of death, that is, the devil;

And deliver them who through fear of death were all their lifetime subject to bondage (Heb. 2:9, 10, 14, 15).

The text here is so descriptive of our Lord. He was made a little lower than the angels, made a man, made like us that by the grace of God He should taste death for every man. In bringing many sons unto glory, the captain of our salvation was made perfect through suffering.

Who in the days of his flesh, when he had offered up prayers and supplications with strong crying and tears unto him that was able to save him from death, and was heard in that he feared;

Though he were a Son, yet learned he obedience by the things which he suffered;

And being made perfect, he became the author of eternal salvation unto all them that obey him (Heb. 5:7-8).

By the grace of God the Captain of our salvation was made "perfect" through suffering. Though He was a son, yet He learned obedience by the things He suffered; and being made "perfect," He became the author of eternal salvation for all of us who will accept Him. To us the word "perfect" means sinless, moral perfection. But it has no connotation like that in the word translated "perfect" (*teleios*).

This word *teleios* refers to a purpose for which a thing was made as being fulfilled. For example, an oak tree is the *teleios* of an acorn. An acorn was made to grow into a tree. So the tree is the *teleios* of the acorn, having achieved the purpose for which the acorn was made. A man is the *teleios* of a boy. If the lad stayed a boy, it would be tragic. He would be stunted. He would not reach the goal for which God made him.

That word is applied to our Lord Christ: it pleased God to make the Captain of our salvation "perfect" through suffering. Though He were a son learning obedience by the things that He suffered, He was made *teleios*, having accomplished the purpose that God planned for Him. He came into the world to suffer and to die in order that having achieved the purpose or *teleios*, He would be the author of an eternal salvation for us who receive His loving grace and the pardon of our sins in Him.

Our Lord Arrives at the Day of His Suffering

In Hebrews 10, there is a magnificent discussion of the purpose (*teleios*) that our Lord achieved for us.

> For it is not possible that the blood of bulls and of goats should take away sins (Heb. 10:4).

Every time sacrifices are made, we are reminded of our sins, according to the author of Hebrews. The sacrifices had to be repeated again and again because they were not able to wash away sins. But our Lord was sacrificed once for all. There is power in the blood.

> Wherefore when he cometh into the world, he saith, Sacrifice and offering thou wouldest not, but a body hast thou prepared me:
> Then said I, Lo, I come (in the volume of the book it is written of me) to do thy will, O God (Heb. 10:5, 7).

He came into the world to fulfill the purpose of God for His life—to suffer, to die that we might be saved.

The gospel poignantly describes the agony of soul in which our Lord faced those days for which He came. As He stood at the threshold of the purpose (*teleios*) to be achieved, i.e., the assignment to suffer, He did it with distress and agony.

In the Gospel of Luke our Lord says,

> But I have a baptism to be baptized with; and how am I straitened [i.e., distressed, in agony] till it be accomplished (12:50).

When the Greeks came to see Him, as recorded in John, it brought to His mind the imminent offering of Himself in suffering for the sins of the whole world.

> Now is my soul troubled; and what shall I say? Father, save me from this hour: but for this cause came I unto this hour (John 12:27).

In Matthew 26, when the disciples sought to defend Him, He said to Simon Peter:

> Put up again thy sword into his place: for all they that take the sword shall perish with the sword.
>
> Thinkest thou that I cannot now pray to my Father, and he shall presently give me more than twelve legions of angels?
>
> But how then shall the scriptures be fulfilled, that thus it must be? (vv. 52-54).

He could have had 72,000 angels standing by His side, but then how would the purpose of God be realized and the scriptural announcement of His coming into the world to die for sins be fulfilled?

> Father, if thou be willing, remove this cup from me: nevertheless not my will, but thine, be done.
>
> And there appeared an angel unto him from heaven, strengthening him.
>
> And being in an agony he prayed more earnestly: and his sweat was as it were great drops of blood falling down to the ground (Luke 22:42-44).

As our Lord entered into His assignment to suffer for our sins, He did so in agony of soul.

In the remarkable prophecy of Isaiah 53, perhaps the greatest prophecy in the Old Testament, the prophet says:

> Yet it pleased the LORD to bruise him; he hath put him to grief: when thou shalt make his soul an offering for sin,
> He shall see of the travail of his soul, and shall be satisfied (vv. 10a, 11a).

God will receive His sacrifice as being sufficient to wash away all our sins.

The prophecy, "God shall see the travail of his soul and shall be satisfied," is beyond my understanding. The travail of the soul of Jesus—God shall make His soul an offering for sin—this is difficult to comprehend. I can understand the crucifixion by reading and by picture, but I do not know how to enter into the travail of soul. As the Lord faced His assignment in suffering, He did so in an agony of spirit that is beyond our comprehension or understanding.

He lived in heaven, where the brightness of holiness resides. But the earth is so filled with death, disease, despair, sorrow, and tears. It must have been a choice of tremendous agony to leave so beautiful a kingdom and to come down to so dark an earth. He did so because we are here, we who are in the agony of death, tears, and sorrow.

Look at Jesus as the Crown Prince of glory. Consider Him as the object of worship of all the angels of heaven.

> And again, when he bringeth in the first begotten into the world, he saith, and let all the angels of God worship him (Heb. 1:6).

So beautiful, resplendent, irridescent, and brilliant was the worship of Jesus in heaven that even Satan, the archangel with whom God entrusted the created world, envied Him. Seeing Jesus as the One before whom all heaven bowed, that sin of pride arose in his heart and led to the destruction of God's universe.

On the other hand, can we imagine the agony of His spirit when they bowed the knee before Him in mockery, saying, "Hail, King of the Jews"? Can we imagine the crown of thorns that was placed on

His head or the scepter made from a cheap reed and placed in His hand or the castoff garment placed on His back as a robe? He who had been the object of the adoration of all the hosts of heaven was now mocked and abused! What agony of soul! I cannot enter into it.

The face of the Son of God is the light and the glory of heaven. They have no need for the sun or the moon, for the light of the Lamb is the brightness of heaven. His face shone as the sun in its splendor. Can you imagine the agony of soul when they covered His face with spittle or when they plucked out His beard or when they smote Him with their hands? The agony of soul of Him who set upon the throne of glory, the God who created the world and who is now nailed to a tree!

In ancient times they impaled their victims. That was their form of execution. In impaling, the victim died immediately. But on the cross, the victim remained for hours and even for days.

The Purpose and Achievement of His Suffering

The author of Hebrews gives three things concerning the suffering of Christ. First, He suffered in order that He might be identified with us and be made one with us.

> For both he that sanctifieth [makes us holy] and they who are sanctified are all of one: for which cause he is not ashamed to call them brethren,
>
> Forasmuch then as the children are partakers of flesh and blood, he also himself likewise took part of the same; that through death he might destroy him that had the power of death, that is, the devil;
>
> For verily he took not on him the nature of angels; but he took on him the seed of Abraham [the likeness of a man].
>
> Wherefore in all things it behooved him to be made like unto his brethren, that he might be a merciful and faithful high priest in things pertaining to God, to make reconciliation for the sins of the people.
>
> For in that he himself hath suffered being tempted, he is able to succor them that are tempted (Heb. 2:11, 14, 16-18).

The first purpose then for the coming of our Lord into the world to suffer was to identify Himself with us. As I think of that, over the long years of my pastoral experience, I do not know of a more common denominator of human life than tears and sorrows and suffering. The common denominator of life is not richness because so many of us are poor. It is not strength and health because so many of us are sick. There is not anything that I know of like the common denominator of suffering, sorrow, and tears. For example, consider the matter of tears as they might affect us in a variety of ways. When the child cries, we say those are childish tears. However, to the child, they are as real as the tears of adults. The broken-heartedness, the disappointment, the hurt, and the sorrow of a child are very real. Consider the tears of teenagers, which express the poignancy of some of the hurt that they go through. Their tears are real. Different still are the tears of manhood and womanhood; the disappointments, the frustrations, the broken dreams that we know in life sometimes crush our souls. The tears of separation, loneliness, old age, and death sometimes bring us to despair.

Jesus came to be made like one of us that we might be one with Him. Had He come into this world as a kingly prince living in a palace with a golden crown and a diamond scepter, how many of us would have felt comfortable in His presence? Had He come into this world as the head of the hosts of brilliant angels, how many of us would have felt that He understands us? But having come into the world poor, the friend of sinners, the meek, the lonely, the hungry, the thirsty, we somehow find Him as our brother. He came to identify Himself with us.

In His obedience, the Scriptures say, though He were a son, He learned submissiveness, carrying out the will of God (Heb. 5:8–9). In so many ways do we need to be taught to be submissive in the harsh providences of life. In submission, Job said:

> Naked came I out of my mother's womb, and naked shall I return thither: the LORD gave, and the LORD hath taken away; blessed be the name of the LORD (Job 1:21).
> Shall we receive good at the hand of God, and shall we not receive evil? In all this did not Job sin with his lips (Job 2:10b).

We see the submissive spirit of our Savior in His words,

The cup which my Father hath given me, shall I not drink it? (John 18:11b).

In His suffering, the Lord is our great sympathizing High Priest. The author of Hebrews says it so beautifully,

> For we have not an high priest which cannot be touched with the feeling of our infirmities; but was in all points tempted like as we are, yet without sin.
> Let us therefore come boldly unto the throne of grace, that we may obtain mercy, and find grace to help in time of need (4:15-16).

He knows all about the sorrow, the frustration, the disappointments, and the tears of our lives. Though He is God, He is our brother. That was the first purpose, the author states, of His coming into the world: that He might identify Himself with us, to be one of us.

The second reason, the author says, for His coming into the world and the purpose (*teleios*) or the achievement of His life was to deliver us from the bondage of death.

> But we see Jesus, who was made a little lower than the angels for the suffering of death, crowned with glory and honor; that he by the grace of God should taste death for every man.
> And deliver them who through fear of death were all their lifetime subject to bondage (Heb 2:9, 15).

All of us have a twofold dread of death. We fear death instinctively. That fear we have in common with all of the animal kingdom. There is no creature that does not seek to escape death by running or fighting. Instinctively we dread the awesome approach of death.

We have another fear of death and that is the uncertainty of what lies beyond death. If one will think of it, it is frightening. What lies in that dark corridor beyond the River Styx, as the Greeks would philosophize about it, beyond *sheol* and its shades, as the Hebrews would say it? What is ahead? What lies beyond the gates of death? Our Savior came to deliver us from that bondage and fear. Because of His victory over death and the grave, we now do not experience death. We are just translated through the open door into heaven. It is God's way of receiving us into paradise. Flesh and blood cannot inherit the kingdom of heaven. As long as I am in this house of clay, I cannot even see God's face and live. Because of Jesus' atoning sacrifice, the victory of Christ means death is but the gate into heaven.

How are those gates wrought and of what are they made? They are gates of pearl, and a pearl is the only gem made out of the hurt and the wound of a little animal. Death is the gate into paradise, into heaven, and it is made out of pearl. Through suffering we enter into the kingdom of God.

During a crusade in Odessa, Texas, a pastor took me to a little coffee shop. While he and I were visiting together, a blind man entered the coffee shop. He came over and sat down close to us, and the pastor said to me, "I want you to listen to that blind man as he prays." Before the man ate, he said the blessing aloud. The pastor said to me, "Every time that blind man prays, he thanks God for his blindness." He went on to explain that before the man was blinded, he had been a very wicked man, but in his blindness he was led to the Lord.

My brothers and sisters, God has some holy purpose for every sorrow that we experience in life. God purposes some beautiful thing for us in it. Instead of rebelling and becoming bitter, let us accept whatever God sends in His providence, and be humbled by it and learn to lean upon the kind arm of God for strength. What is heaven like? It is described as being a place where there is no more death or sorrow or crying. Neither will there be any more pain or tears, for these things have all passed away. What would that mean to someone who had never cried? What would that mean to someone who had never suffered? What would that mean to someone whose heart had never been broken? What would that mean to someone who had never faced death? It is in these providences of God in which our Savior is a brother that we come to know the riches of the depth and the height and the breadth of the love of God in Christ Jesus. That is why He came to suffer.

There is a third reason for His suffering:

But we see Jesus, who was made a little lower than the angels for the suffering of death, crowned with glory and honor; that he by the grace of God should taste death for every man.

For it became him, for whom are all things, and by whom are all things, in bringing many sons unto glory, to make the captain of their salvation perfect through sufferings (Heb. 2:9-10).

Do you see the imagery of that? The great throng that our Lord is leading into heaven is a throng that He has saved by virtue of His tears, suffering, and death. It is a sainted throng that He is leading into glory. Every pilgrim company must have a "Great Heart." Every army must have a general or a captain. Every exodus must have a Moses. Leading the saints of God into heaven, we have the great Savior and Captain of our salvation.

In Ephesians we read about a magnificent imagery comparing the entrance of our Lord with His people into heaven to a Roman triumph.

When he ascended up on high, he led captivity captive, and gave gifts unto men (4:8).

Satan is chained to his chariot wheels, and accompanying the Lord into glory are the saints He has won, the people for whom He has died, the souls whom He has saved. In that great throng going into heaven there are the sinners, the blind, the crippled, the hurt, the sorrowing, the weeping, the repentant. These are the saints whom the Lord is taking with Him into glory.

In my reading, I came across something that blessed my heart. It is about an American doctor. Though his name is not given in the book, his funeral is described. The article said that when he was buried, the funeral carriage that carried him was attended by sixty pallbearers, each one of whom owed his life to that beloved physician. Behind the pallbearer's carriages walked eight hundred men, all of whom owed their ability to walk to the ministries of that beloved doctor. An additional 293 carriages followed. This was not the funeral of a great military hero or a political genius, but it was the memorial service of a man of God who had poured his life into the healing of the people. That is going to be the way it is when God leads His saints marching into heaven. These are they whom He has lifted out of the gutter. These are they whom He has pardoned from their sins. These are they to whom He has given strength, health, hope, life, and salvation. They are going to follow our Lord into heaven. The author here speaks of it as "leading many sons into glory."

O Lord, what a wonderful, incomparably precious thing God has done in sending us His beloved and only Son! Identified with us, sympathizing with us, taking away from us the fear of the agony of death, and opening for us the gates of glory through which one day we shall follow Him, marching into heaven!

5
The Cross and the Crown

(Isa. 53:10-12)

> Yet it pleased the LORD to bruise him; he hath put him to grief: when thou shalt make his soul an offering for sin, he shall see his seed, he shall prolong his days, and the pleasure of the LORD shall prosper in his hand.
>
> He shall see of the travail of his soul, and shall be satisfied: by his knowledge shall my righteous servant justify many; for he shall bear their iniquities.
>
> Therefore will I divide him a portion with the great, and he shall divide the spoil with the strong; because he hath poured out his soul unto death: and he was numbered with the transgressors; and he bare the sin of many, and made intercession for the transgressors (Isa. 53:10-12).

In chapter 53 we find bound together the humiliation and exaltation of our Lord. Typical of the prophets as they spoke of His coming, Isaiah wrote:

> He was oppressed, and he was afflicted, yet he opened not his mouth: he is brought as a lamb to the slaughter, and as a sheep before her shearers is dumb, so he openeth not his mouth. . . .
>
> Therefore will I divide him a portion with the great, and he shall divide the spoil with the strong. (vv. 53:7, 12a)

The same marvelous depiction of our Savior as being humble and exalted is found in the apostles. Typical of the presentation is the passage of Scripture found in Philippians:

> Let this mind be in you, which was also in Christ Jesus:
> Who, being in the form of God, thought it not robbery to be equal with God:

But made himself of no reputation, and took upon him the form of a servant, and was made in the likeness of men:

And being found in fashion as a man, he humbled himself, and became obedient unto death, even the death of the cross.

Wherefore God also hath highly exalted him, and given him a name which is above every name:

That at the name of Jesus every knee should bow, of things in heaven, and things in earth, and things under the earth;

And that every tongue should confess that Jesus Christ is Lord, to the glory of God the Father. (2:5-11)

In Revelation John says:

And when I saw him, I fell at his feet as dead. And he laid his right hand upon me, saying unto me, Fear not; I am the first and the last.

I am he that liveth, and was dead; and, behold, I am alive for evermore, Amen; and have the keys of hell and of death. (1:17, 18)

And I beheld, and I heard the voice of many angels round about the throne and the beasts and the elders: and the number of them was ten thousand times ten thousand, and thousands of thousands;

Saying with a loud voice, Worthy is the Lamb that was slain to receive power, and riches, and wisdom, and strength, and honour, and glory, and blessing.

And every creature which is in heaven, and on the earth, and under the earth, and such as are in the sea, and all that are in them, heard I saying, Blessing, and honour, and glory, and power, and unto him that sitteth upon the throne, and unto the Lamb for ever and ever. (5:11-13)

The Suffering Lamb

Our highest imagination cannot enter into the glory nor comprehend the exaltation from whence He came. The immeasurable distance between the glory of our Lord in heaven and the shame to which He descended in earth is beyond human understanding. He was made in the form of a man who is composed of the dust of the ground. He became a servant. Finally, our Lord was sentenced to execution in a death reserved for criminals and felons. He was raised between the heaven and the earth as though both heaven and earth rejected Him.

As though abuse were not vile enough, the cruel jeering crowd covered Him with spittle. They also plucked out His beard. Going further, they crowned Him with thorns, and as though the thorns were not agonizing enough, He was pierced through with a Roman spear. It was the earth's saddest hour and it was humanity's deepest, darkest day. At 3:00 P.M. it was all over. The Lord of life bowed His head and the light of the world flickered out.

Tread softly around the cross, for Jesus is dead. Repeat the refrain in hushed and softened tone. The Lord of life is dead. The lips that spoke forth Lazarus from the grave are now stilled in the silence of the death. The head that was anointed by Mary of Bethany is bowed with its crown of thorns. The eyes that wept over Jerusalem are glazed in death. The hands that blessed little children are nailed to a tree. The feet that walked on the waters of blue Galilee are fastened to a cross. The heart that went out in compassionate love and sympathy for the poor and the lost of the world is now broken. He is dead.

The infuriated mob that cried for His crucifixion gradually disperses. He is dead. The passersby who stopped just to see Him, go on their way. He is dead. The Pharisees, rubbing their hands in self-congratulation, go back to the city. He is dead. The Sadducees, breathing sighs of relief, return to their coffers in the temple. He is dead. The centurion who was assigned the task of executing Him makes his official report to the Roman procurator, "He is dead." The soldiers who were sent to dispatch the victim, and seeing the man on the center cross was certainly dead, broke not His bones but pierced Him through. He is dead. Joseph of Arimathaea and Nicodemus of the Sanhedrin go to Pontius Pilate and beg the Roman governor for His body because He is dead. Mary, His mother, and the women with her are bowed in sobs and tears. He is dead. The eleven apostles, like frightened sheep, crawl into eleven shadows to hide from the pointing finger of Jerusalem and they cry that He is dead. Wherever His disciples meet, the same refrain is sadly heard: He is dead. It would be almost impossible for us to enter into the depths of despair that gripped their hearts. Simon Peter, "the Rock," is a rock no longer. James and John are "sons of thunder" no longer. Simon the Zealot is a zealot no longer. Jesus is dead. The hope of the world has perished with Him.

He Is Alive!

Then men stopped dead in their tracks. A message leaps from mouth to mouth like liquid fire. An angel says, "He is alive!" Mary Magdalene says, "I have seen the Lord!" Simon Peter is filling Jerusalem with the bold and courageous announcement: "He is alive, He is alive!" All up and down the highways of Judaea, along the shores of Galilee, beyond the coasts of the great Mediterranean, on the road to Athens and Rome, in every poor man's cottage and in every rich man's palace, there is that glorious news: "He is alive, He is alive!"

> Lift up your heads ye sorrowing ones,
> And be ye glad of heart.
> For earth's saddest day and earth's gladdest day,
> Calvary's day and Easter day are just one day apart.

The bitter seed brought forth a beautiful and precious flower. The cross magnifies our exalted and risen Lord. Every point in that crown of thorns is now a diamond in His diadem. The crimson of His life that was poured out stained His royal robe with purple. The iron nails of the cross and of the spear are now the rod of His scepter by which He will rule the nations of the world. The wood of the cross is His identity with all humanity. The most sacred spot in the earth is Mount Calvary where He died. The cross itself is the symbol of the Christian faith and our hope in the world that is to come.

> If in Flanders' fields poppies grow,
> It will be between crosses row on row.

If He is alive, where is He now? There are almost two thousand years of the record of His living. Is there proof? Is there evidence? Had every man in the Roman Empire seen Him walk out of that grave, had Caesar and all of his officers witnessed the resurrection of Christ on the first day of the week, had Josephus, Tacitus, and Suetonius recorded in their historical annals the eyewitnesses of the living Lord, it would not be proof as corroborated as the evidence that we have today in our very lives.

How We Know He Lives

First, we know His presence by His healing grace and His saving power. The only healing is divine healing. A surgeon may sharpen his scalpel and cut, but only God can heal. Jesus is the Great Physician. In how many sick rooms, darkened in despair, have we seen health, life, and length of days given in the gracious and healing hands of our living Lord!

Second, He is alive because He bows down His ear to hear His children when they pray. Without number are the times when we laid before our blessed Lord those decisions, problems, and hurts for which we are not equal in our lives. We told Him all about it. He, who was tried in all points such as we, has bowed down His ear in sympathy and understanding to hear His children when they pray. He is alive. I know Him in answered prayer.

Third, the ableness of His might to regenerate, to save, to deliver, to forgive, and to make new men and women can easily be seen. I see His power in the glorious conversions that daily are brought to God, trophies of grace under His saving hand. They are a Simon Peter, a Paul the persecuting blasphemer of the early Christians, an Ignatius who was fed to the lions in the Roman colosseum, a Billy Sunday, and a George W. Truett. Christ moves in saving power today to save you and me as He did yesterday; He is able just the same.

Fourth, He lives as He walks in grace and blessing among His churches. In Revelation 1 we read:

> And I turned to see the voice that spake with me. And being turned, I saw seven golden candlesticks;
> And in the midst of the seven candlesticks one like unto the Son of man, clothed with a garment down to the foot, and girt about the paps with a golden girdle. (vv. 12, 13)

Christ walks among His people, visiting in His churches. There have been times without number when seated in my pulpit chair, I have bowed my head with tears overflowing in the sense of the presence of the power of Christ in this holy place. Our Lord can be found in the midst of His churches.

Fifth, He lives in the victory that He has brought to us over death. "Be not afraid, for I have the keys of the grave and of death." Lest one might think that those keys lie in some other hand, He avows that He possesses the key to our lives and to our deaths. I shall not die until He wills my death. Flame or sword, famine or plague cannot touch me until He appoints the time. Nor am I to cringe before the visage of that pale visitor, death, for our Lord went to the cross and there He destroyed our enemy death and forever brings victory and triumph out of the tomb. There is no sting in death nor victory in the grave, for Christ has made death for us our entrance into heaven. When I die will be in His all-powerful choice. Death to the Christian holds no terror, for death is but a homegoing to be with Jesus.

"Yea, though I walk through the valley of the shadow of death, I will fear no evil: for thou art with me." The hour of our death is to be our greatest day. It is our moment of triumph, when earth recedes and heaven draws near, first the cross and then the crown.

> O precious cross,
> O glorious crown,
> O resurrection day,
> Ye angels from the stars come down,
> And bear my soul away.

This is the victory Christ has brought us in His precious, nail-pierced hands.

6
Christ Died for Our Sins

(1 Cor. 15:1-3)

> Moreover, brethren, I declare unto you the gospel which I preached
> unto you, which also ye have received, and wherein ye stand; by
> which also ye are saved, if ye keep in memory what I preached unto
> you, unless ye have believed in vain. For I delivered unto you first of
> all that which I also received, how that Christ died for our sins accord-
> ing to the scriptures (1 Corinthians 15:1-3).

"CHRIST DIED FOR OUR SINS according to the scriptures." This is the
third great affirmation of the Bible. After the primeval declaration of
the existence and creative workmanship of Almighty God and after
the declaration that Jesus Christ is the Messiah, the Son of the
Blessed, this is the third great affirmation—that the Son of God died
in our behalf according to the Word of the Lord.

There are two kinds of Christianity. There is a Christianity merely
of ideals and inspiration and good works, an ethical and social
Christianity. In this system Christ is preached as a mighty teacher
and leader and example and humanitarian. He is presented as a noble reformer and martyr. It is the Christianity of inspiration and im-
provement. If its disciples use the word "*salvation*," this is what they
mean by it—personal and social amelioration. Confucius was a great
teacher, contributing to the social order. Socrates was a great
teacher, contributing to the social order. Aurelius and Justinian were
great teachers, contributing to the social order. Jesus, also, is a great
teacher, contributing to the social order. This is the Christianity of
inspiration and good works.

But there is also another kind of Christianity. It is the Christianity
of redemption. It preaches the heaven-born Gospel that God in

glory was moved in mercy and love by the tragic plight of the lost human race and that He gave His Son to die in our stead. On the cruel and merciless Cross, He took our place as our substitute and died for our sins, that we might be delivered from the terrible judgment and penalty which was our just due because of our iniquities. This Gospel announces the glad tidings that, through faith in this atoning Christ, we are forgiven, we are restored, we are justified, we are saved. It announces the glorious truth that a redeemed man is a regenerated man, a new creation, one who has died with his Lord to the world and has been raised with his Lord to walk in newness of life. It proclaims the startling and burning fact that the good works of the Christian are in no wise an attempt to merit the way of heaven, but are rendered unto God out of a heart of gratitude for what Christ has done for a lost and helpless sinner.

In the first kind of Christianity (the Christianity of ideals and inspiration and good works, the ethical and social Christianity), the death of Christ is but an incident, though a moving devotion. In the second kind of Christianity (the Christianity of redemption), the death of Christ is the cardinal truth around which all other truths revolve. In the first kind of Christianity, if one takes away the death of Christ, the system is not particularly disturbed. In fact, many of its exponents would rather like to get rid of the blood and suffering of the old-time message. The offense of the Cross has become too great. I held a revival meeting one time in a church that used hymnbooks from which had been purged every song of the so-called "bloody gospel." It insulted their sophisticated intelligence to sing, "There is a fountain filled with blood," even though the hymn was written by one of England's greatest poets. In the Christianity of redemption, however, if one takes away the death of Christ, he takes away the forgiveness of sin, the hope of heaven, and the promise of the world to come.

The Christianity of the Cross

Which of these two is the Christianity of the New Testament? According to the third great affirmation of the Word of God, it is the Christianity of redemption, the Christianity of the Cross. It is the "bloody gospel" in all its naked hideousness, as the Roman would have it; in all its philosophic irrationality, as the Greek would have it; in all its shame and offense and suffering, as Paul describes it. The Christianity of blood atonement is the Christianity of the Book—"according to the scriptures."

In the text I Corinthians 15:3, Paul says: "For I delivered unto you first of all." "First of all." Not first in time but first in importance. As there is a first and great commandment of the law, so there is a first and great doctrine of the New Testament. It is not the doctrine of the Fatherhood of God, or the doctrine of the Kingdom of Heaven, or the doctrine of the Incarnation of Jesus, but it is the doctrine of the Atonement of Christ. The doctrine of the vicarious expiation of our sins by the death of Christ is the very keynote of grace, the very heart of the message from heaven. No other doctrine stands so high. No other doctrine is so pervasively and prevailingly central. I stood one day in the ruins of the Roman Forum, at the place where was located the golden milestone, and I remembered the ancient saying, "All roads lead to Rome." From that golden milestone, every road was measured to the farthest ends of the empire. It is thus with the cardinal, central doctrine of the Cross. All truths lead to the Cross and from the Cross flow out those streams of unmeasured mercy that reach to the farthest ends of the earth. An unsympathetic critic one time said to the famous London preacher, Charles Haddon Spurgeon: "All your sermons are alike." Spurgeon instantly replied: "Yes, indeed, they are. I take a text anywhere in the Bible and immediately I make a beeline for the Cross."

The whole story of the whole Bible is the story of Jesus, and the story of Jesus centers around the day of His Cross. It is the scarlet thread that binds the ages together and to Him. There is no pardon without atonement. There is no remission without shedding of blood. There is no reconciliation without payment of debt. Not by the purity and holiness of His life, but by His stripes we are healed. Such events as the birth of Jesus, His temptation, His transfiguration, His institution of the Lord's Supper, even His ascension into heaven, are absent from one or more of the gospels. But they all in fullest detail relate the story of His suffering and death.

This is the distinctive, determining doctrine of the New Testament Scriptures, a doctrine which distinguishes the Christian faith from all other religions. The Christian religion is distinctly a religion of redemption. Its fundamental purpose is to recover man from the bondage and judgment of sin. The Christian faith is not in the first place an ethic, although it is ethical. It is not in the first place a theology, although it has a theology. It is not in the first place reformational, although it has social, cultural, and political overtones. The Christian faith is first and above all a Gospel of redemption, an announcement of the good news that God for Christ's sake has forgiven sinful men. The symbol of the Christian church is not a burning bush; it is not a table of stone; it is not a seven-branch lampstand; it is not a halo around a submissive head; it is not a crown of splendid triumph. It is a cross—rugged and naked—a heavy, wooden cross. Here is the spectacle for men and angels to behold in wonder and amazement. Here is God's eternal sign to which the sinner can look for salvation and to which the saint can look for confidence and strength.

> There is life for a look at the crucified One.
>   There is life at this moment for thee.
> Then look, sinner, look unto Him and be saved,
>   Unto Him who was nailed to the tree.

> Have you been to Jesus for the cleansing power?
>   Are you washed in the blood of the Lamb?
> Are you freely trusting in His grace this hour?
>   Are you washed in the blood of the Lamb?

> Oh, precious is the flow
>   That makes me white as snow.
> No other fount I know—
>   Nothing but the blood of Jesus.

The Scriptures and the Cross

In the text Paul affirms that Christ died for our sins "according to the scriptures." "According to the scriptures" as "the Lamb slain from the foundation of the world" (Revelation 13:8). The Apostle

Peter writes: "Who verily was foreordained before the foundation of the world, but was manifest in these last times for you" (I Peter 1:20).

The burden of the Old Testament scriptures is the atonement of Christ. The blood shed in the Garden of Eden to hide the shame and nakedness of our first parents spoke of Jesus. The sacrifice of Abel spoke of Jesus. The offering up of Isaac, Abraham's son of promise, spoke of Jesus. The Passover lamb ("When I see the blood, I will pass over you") spoke of Jesus. The Levitical offerings and sacrifices spoke of Jesus. "For the life of the flesh is in the blood: and I have given it to you upon the altar to make an atonement for your souls: for it is the blood that maketh an atonement for the soul" (Leviticus 17:11). The daily sacrifice in the temple spoke of Jesus. "Without shedding of blood, there is no remission of sins." The message of the prophets spoke of Jesus. "But he was wounded for our transgressions, he was bruised for our iniquities: the chastisement of our peace was upon him; and with his stripes we are healed. All we like sheep have gone astray; we have turned every one to his own way; and the LORD hath laid on him the iniquity of us all. Yet it pleased the LORD to bruise him; he hath put him to grief: when thou shalt make his soul an offering for sin, he shall see his seed, he shall prolong his days, and the pleasure of the Lord shall prosper in his hand. He shall see of the travail of his soul, and shall be satisfied: by his knowledge shall my righteous servant justify many; for he shall bear their iniquities" (Isaiah 53:5-6, 10-11).

The burden of the New Testament is the message of the atonement of Christ. The keynote of the whole gospel story is sounded by John the Baptist in his introduction of our Lord: "Behold the Lamb of God, which taketh away the sin of the world" (John 1:29). The four gospels proclaim this message of redemption in their very form. They are not biographies of Jesus. They are selected words and incidents. "And many other signs truly did Jesus in the presence of his disciples, which are not written in this book" (John 20:30). "And there are also many other things which Jesus did, the which, if they should be written every one, I suppose that even the world itself could not contain the books that should be written" (John 21:25).

And yet, even though the four gospels are but a few selections out of so very much that entered into the life of our Lord, fully one-fourth of the space of the gospels is given over to the last few days, in fact, to the last few hours of His life. A thousand interesting events of His career are passed over, a thousand marvelous discourses are never mentioned, in order to leave room for the story of His death.

As soon as our Lord begins His public ministry, He refers to His coming death. "Jesus answered and said unto them, Destroy this temple, and in three days I will raise it up" (John 2:19). The temple authorities did not understand His saying, but we do. When Nicodemus came to Jesus by night, in the first days of our Lord's ministry, the Saviour spoke to him about the serpent raised in the wilderness. "And as Moses lifted up the serpent in the wilderness, even so must the Son of man be lifted up: that whosoever believeth in him should not perish, but have eternal life" (John 3:14, 15). Nicodemus did not understand Him, but we do. In the unfolding ministry of our Lord through the days and years that followed His coming, atoning death was referred to again and again. In His sermon in the synagogue at Capernaum to the Jews, who were already striving among themselves, He further astonished His auditors by declaring: "Verily, verily, I say unto you, Except ye eat the flesh of the Son of man and drink his blood, ye have no life in you. Whoso eateth my flesh, and drinketh my blood, hath eternal life; and I will raise him up at the last day. For my flesh is meat indeed, and my blood is drink indeed. He that eateth my flesh, and drinketh my blood, dwelleth in me, and I in him. As the living Father hath sent me, and I live by the Father: so He that eateth me, even he shall live by me. This is that bread which came down from heaven: not as your fathers did eat manna, and are dead: he that eateth of this bread shall live forever" (John 6:53-58).

When the Greeks came to see Him at Jerusalem, their visit precipitated a conflict in His deepest soul as He was brought face to face once again with His atoning death for the sins of all the world. "And there were certain Greeks among them that came up to worship at the feast: The same came therefore to Philip, which was of Bethsaida of Galilee, and desired him, saying, Sir, we would see Jesus. Philip cometh and telleth Andrew: and again Andrew and Philip tell Jesus. And Jesus answered them, saying, The hour is come, that the Son of man should be glorified. Verily, verily, I say unto you, Except a corn of wheat fall into the ground and die, it abideth alone: but if it die, it bringeth forth much fruit. He that loveth his life shall lose it; and he that hateth his life in this world shall keep it unto life eternal. . . . Now is my soul troubled; and what shall I say? Father, save me from this hour: but for this cause came I unto this hour. Father, glorify thy name. Then came there a voice from heaven, saying, I have both glorified it, and will glorify it again. The people therefore, that stood by, and heard it, said that it thundered: others said, An angel spake to him. Jesus answered and said, This voice came not because of me, but for your sakes. Now is the judgment of this world: now shall the prince of this world be cast out. And I, if I be lifted up from the earth, will draw all men unto me. This he said, signifying what death he should die" (John 12:20-33). When Mary anointed Him at the feast in Bethany, it was, according to His own words, "against the day of my burying."

The recurring memorial, the institution of the Lord's Supper, is forever to focus our attention upon His atoning death on the Cross. Christ worked many miracles, yet He never said: "This miracle is wrought for the remission of sins." Christ healed many sick, yet He never said: "This healing is bestowed for the remission of sins." Christ preached many sermons, but He never said: "This sermon is delivered for the remission of sins." Christ was tempted and transfigured, yet He never said: "This temptation is borne and this transfiguration is achieved for the remission of sins." But our Lord did say, "This is my blood of the new covenant, shed for the remission of sins." The heart of the Gospel is the story of the day of the Cross.

The burden of the preaching of the apostles is the atoning death of our Saviour. In the shadow of the Cross they stood to preach. Paul fervently declared, "God forbid that I should glory, save in the cross of our Lord Jesus Christ" (Galatians 6:14). In the New Testament they left behind, every leaf and every word is inspired by His suffering and stained by His blood. "For I determined not to know any thing among you, save Jesus Christ, and him crucified" (I Corinthians 2:2). "I am crucified with Christ, nevertheless I live; yet not I, but Christ liveth in me: and the life which I now live in the flesh I live by the faith of the Son of God, who loved me, and gave himself for me" (Galatians 2:20). "The blood of Jesus Christ his Son cleanseth us from all sin" (I John 1:7). "And he is the propitiation for our sins: and not for ours only, but also for the sins of the whole world" (I John 2:2). "Unto Him that loved us, and washed us from our sins in his own blood, and hath made us kings and priests unto God and his Father; to him be glory and dominion for ever and ever" (Revelation 1:5-6).

What Do You See, When You Look at the Cross?

Our gospel message of hope and salvation today centers in the Cross of our Lord Jesus Christ. What do you see when you look at the Cross? The Roman soldiers looked and they saw garments to be coveted and a robe for which to gamble. The priests looked and they saw an enemy to be destroyed. The curious passers-by, who sat down and watched Him there, saw a scene in which to idle away a weary hour. One malefactor looked and saw another criminal, like himself, being crucified. The other thief looked and saw hope for heaven: "Lord, remember me when thou comest into thy kingdom." The centurion looked and said: "Surely this man was the Son of God." The ruler of the Passover feast looked and saw a polluted body that had to be removed before the Sabbath Day drew on. Pilate's quaternion of soldiers looked and were commissioned with three deaths to be ascertained. Two of the three certainly expired with the breaking of their bones by heavy mallets, and the other was declared certainly dead with a spear, opening His heart and His side. John looked and saw a fountain of blood and water for atonement and cleansing of our sins. Joseph of Arimathaea and Nicodemus looked and saw a precious body to be lovingly laid away. God, the Father, looked and saw the sacrifice of His only-begotten Son.

When you look upon the Cross, what do you see? When Jesus stands before you, upon His brow the crown of thorns, mocked, rejected, scourged, bleeding, dying, what do you feel? Surely, surely we are conscience-stricken, for His suffering is a revelation of the judgment of God upon the sin of our own hearts. It is our sins that placed upon His brow the crown of thorns. It is our sins that laid upon His back the cruel and heavy stripes. It is our sins that nailed Him to the tree. A man once dreamed that he stood in the soldiers' hall of the palace of Pontius Pilate and saw one of the legionaries scourge our Lord. As the Roman soldier laid upon the back of the unresisting Saviour the thick, heavy lash, studded with jagged pieces of lead, the blood streamed from the welts that were made. When the soldier lifted His hand to strike again, the dreamer could no longer bear the sorrow of those inflicted wounds. He rushed forward to seize the hand of the soldier. When the soldier in astonishment turned around, the dreamer recognized himself! Surely it is our sins that we see in the sufferings of His Cross, in His tears, in His sorrows, in His wounds, and in His death.

When you look at the Cross, what do you see? Do you see the love of God for a lost humanity? "For God so loved the world, that he gave his only begotten Son, that whosoever believeth in him should not perish, but have everlasting life" (John 3:16). "For he hath made him to be sin for us, who knew no sin; that we might be made the righteousness of God in him" (I Corinthians 5:21). He died in our stead. It is by the love of God for us that we are delivered from so terrible a penalty.

When you look upon the Cross, what do you see? Do you see our victory over sin and death and the grave? Through the torn veil of His flesh, we have our entrance into heaven. "Having therefore, brethren, boldness to enter into the holiest by the blood of Jesus, by a new and living way, which he hath consecrated for us, through the veil, that is to say, his flesh" (Hebrews 10:19-20).

When you look at the Cross, do you hear God's call to the human heart? Do you not feel God's entreaty to your own soul?

> When I survey the wondrous cross
> On which the Prince of glory died,

My richest gain I count but loss,
  And pour contempt on all my pride.

Forbid it, Lord, that I should boast,
  Save in the death of Christ, my God!
All the vain things that charm me most,
  I sacrifice them to His blood.

See, from His head, His hands, His feet.
  Sorrow and love flow mingled down;
Did e'er such love and sorrow meet,
  Or thorns compose so rich a crown?

Were the whole realm of nature mine,
  That were a present far too small;
Love so amazing, so divine,
  Demands my soul, my life, my all.

Somehow when we truly see the meaning of the death of Jesus, the world is never the same again. Our hearts are never the same again, and the path of our lives can no longer follow the old course and the worldly way.

The very message of God, a call to repentance and dedication, is found in the Cross of our Saviour. Long ago young Count Zinzendorf was a playboy who revelled in the use of his riches and nobility for worldly and selfish purposes. One day in the art gallery of Dusseldorf, he looked long and steadfastly upon an *ecce homo*, a picture of the suffering Saviour. Underneath the moving portrait were these words:

> *Hoc feci pro te,*
> *Quid facis pro me?*
> (This I have done for thee,
> What hast thou done for me?)

The young nobleman turned from that sight of our suffering Lord to devote his life and his fortune to the propagation of the Gospel, a dedication that, through the founding of modern missionary movements, has reached in loving and saving power to the farthest, darkest corners of the earth. It is thus with us all. The picture of Christ, crucified before our very eyes, compels us in God's moving and loving power to kneel at His feet, to look up into His face, to turn from our sins and to ask the mercy and forgiveness of Heaven in His blessed and saving name. This is the power of the Cross and of the Son of God who "died for our sins according to the scriptures."

7
The Beginning of Grace
(Gen. 3:8-9)

> They heard the voice of the Lord God walking in the garden. . . .
> And the Lord God called unto Adam, and said unto him, Where art
> thou? (Gen. 3:8-9).

Someone has said that the saddest sentence God ever uttered is
this, "Adam, where art thou?" Heretofore the man and the woman
had met the Lord with heavenly eagerness. They were a happy, innocent pair, and it was always a glad, glorious hour when Jehovah
came to talk with them. They had no fear. But now something griev-
ous and sorrowful has happened. The man is afraid. Both are
ashamed. And the Lord calls with a sob in His voice, "O Adam,
where art thou, and what hast thou done?" The answer to that
heartbroken question is the whole story of sin and grace and atonement.

The Grief of God

A wise and experienced homiletics professor, teaching his class of
young ministers the art of preaching, called upon each one to read
this section of the book of Genesis. As each student stood up to read
the passage, the old professor was watchfully waiting. Some read it
as though God were simply asking a question, "Adam, where art
thou?" Some read it as though God were angry. Some read it as
though he were indifferent. But one young preacher read it in pa-
thos, with a sob in his voice, "And the Lord God called unto Adam,
and said unto him, Where art thou?"

The old professor looked at the youth searchingly and said,
"Young man, you will be a great evangelist. God has given you a

compassion for the souls of men. When God came into the garden in the cool of the day and called to the man He had made, God was brokenhearted as He asked where he was and what he had done."

"But," one may inquire, "didn't the Lord God know about the possibility of the fall before He made the man? Did He not foresee this transgression and guilt? Then how could the grief of God be sincere and genuine?" It is a reasonable query, and its answer can be found in the hearts of fathers and mothers who rear their children in this world. They send them out to live lives of their own, all the while knowing that in their going forth they must face temptation which may prove stronger than they can resist. If their children fall, is the grief of the parents none the less true and sincere because of their foreknowledge? No, no, indeed! Their hearts are still broken when they learn that one of their own has succumbed to the wiles of Satan.

The Beginning of Sin

Said the Evil One to our first parents, "Yea, hath God said, Ye shall not eat of every tree of the garden?" Sin began with a question mark, the questioning of God's word. The woman repeated the word of the Lord: "We may eat of the fruit of the trees of the garden: but of the fruit of the tree which is in the midst of the garden, God hath said, Ye shall not eat of it, neither shall ye touch it, lest ye die." Then followed the first lie. "And the serpent said unto the woman, Ye shall not surely die."

This is the way of the archfiend. He whispers in our hearts, "Yea, doth God say—? God doth not say the truth." Satan always places an interrogation point after God's word. The father of lies says: "Does God say in His Word, 'Except ye repent of your sins and trust in the Lord, you will certainly die'? Yea, does God say that?" Then Satan answers in our hearts, "Ye shall not die." "Yea," says Satan, "does God say in His book, 'Thou shalt surely die, thou shalt be lost, lost in hell, forever doomed, shut out from heaven'? Does God say that?" Then Satan sweetly whispers: "Nay, God does not tell the truth. There is no second death, there is no hell, there is no final judgment, there is no condemnation. God is trying to scare you; He does not tell you what is true."

God says, "Except ye repent, ye shall all likewise perish." But Satan denies, "Nay, God does not tell you the truth. Repentance is an antiquated idea. You can be saved without repentance." God says, "There is none other name under heaven given among men, whereby we must be saved." But Satan denies: "Nay, God is not so strict or straightlaced. He will save all men, whatever they believe; consequently, belief in Christ Jesus is optional. You can be saved without faith in Christ." Thus does Satan blind the hearts of men and hurl their souls into hell.

The Beginning of Grace

The grace of God began in the heart of God. The Lord looked upon this man He had made, a man rebellious, a man who had rather follow the seductive whisperings of the serpent than to heed the word of life. What should God have done in that terrible day of transgression? Surely, not love the transgressor all the more!

The man refused to say: "God shall be my all in all. His Word shall be my light and my life. I will obey His voice. I will walk in His commandments." No! The man God made rebelled and said: "I will not obey. I will not walk in the way. God said not to touch this thing, but I will touch it. He said not to eat, but I will eat." In a rebellious spirit he transgressed God's commandment.

Now, what should God have done? As I reread the story, the thought comes to my heart, why didn't God destroy him? Why didn't God annihilate him? Why didn't God then and there crush him into the dust of the earth; pour him back into that ground out of which he was made?

That same thought comes with overwhelming force as I view the world scene today. All flesh seems to exhibit the same spirit of rebellion and transgression. Men following the counsels of Satan bring upon the world a misery and despair that cry in agony unto heaven. Why doesn't God reach down out of heaven and destroy the warmongers? Why doesn't God eradicate communism? Why doesn't

God hurl down out of His heaven those thunderbolts that would subvert the agitators who are ruining the hopes and dreams for the peace of the world? Why do wicked men still live in the presence of the Almighty who rules heaven and earth?

In one of a series of memorial services held for our brave young men who were killed across the waters in World War II, the body of one of our finest Christian boys lay on the cemetery green, ready for reburial, as his dear father and mother and little sister sat near by, sobbing their hearts out. And I thought: "O God, what of this needless sacrifice? O God, why don't you reach down and take out of this world, all the wicked people who cause such tears and anguish and heartache?" I think the same thing here when I read of the first transgression. "Lord God, why didn't You stretch forth Your hand and destroy that first sinning couple for disobeying Your commandment and refusing to walk in Your way?"

But no! For the first time the heart of God is revealed, and the occasion of that revelation is the sin and transgression of our first parents. The reason God did not destroy them is that He is a God of mercy, of kindness, of love; not willing that any should perish but that all should come to repentance. Heretofore we have known God as the mighty Creator. Until we come to the third chapter of Genesis, the Lord God is revealed as one of might, one of great creative power. In the third chapter of the book we see a new Lord and a new God. He is the Lord of mercy, of love, of forgiveness. He is the God of grace.

God is more than creative power, infinite authority, and potential judgment. He is all that, but He is more. God has a heart, and that heart goes out in love and kindness for the man He has made. "And the Lord God formed man of the dust of the ground." That was power. "And the Lord God called unto Adam and said unto him, Where art thou?" That was grace—the seeking God, the shepherd heart, the father who waits and prays for the prodigal! No one can say what God sees in the lost sinner nor how much He loves him. Eternity alone will reveal it. But we know that, to God, one lost soul is worth every drop of blood on Calvary, every tear and grief of the Saviour's life. Would God have sent His Son to redeem the material

world? A universe? A thousand universes? No, we think not. But
He did send His Son to die for you and me that we might be redeemed from our sins. Oh, the depth of the love and grace and
mercy of God!

> Marvelous grace of our living Lord,
>   Grace that exceeds our sin and our guilt,
> Yonder on Calvary's mount outpoured,
>   There where the blood of the Lamb was spilt.
>
> Grace, grace, God's grace,
>   Grace that will pardon and cleanse within;
> Grace, grace, God's grace,
>   Grace that is greater than all our sin.

The Way of Redemption

Now we come to the merciful plan of redemption, the way of salvation announced here in the beginning of God's Book. It is called
the "protevangelium," "the first gospel," and this is it: "And the
Lord God said unto the serpent, . . . I will put enmity between thee
and the woman, and between thy seed and her seed; it shall bruise
thy head, and thou shalt bruise his heel." "And the seed of the
woman shall bruise the serpent's head." Ah, how much, how much,
when we come to know what finally and fully that meant! It meant
Calvary; it meant the blood of the cross. It meant the coming of Jesus
into the world. It meant the crown of thorns and the atoning blood in
the hill called the "place of a skull." It was through the deception of
the woman that sin came into the world. It was through the concep-
tion of the woman, the seed of the woman, the Son of Mary, that
redemption was brought to the fallen race. This "protevangelium"
was the first announcement of the glorious message of the gospel of
hope,

This same gospel of blood-bought redemption is prefigured in the
twenty-first verse of the third chapter of Genesis: "Unto Adam also
and to his wife did the Lord God make coats of skins, and clothed
them." When the man found himself naked, and his wife, they
sewed fig leaves together that they might hide their shame. "And

the eyes of them both were opened, and they knew that they were naked; and they sewed fig leaves together, and made themselves aprons." This is a profound impulse in the human heart. All of us have tried to hide away, to cover out of sight the sin and guilt of our lives. But we cannot do it; fig leaves will not cover it up. One reason a desperately wicked man is sometimes a leader in some of the noble philanthropies and charities of the community is because he seeks to cover up the hideousness, the gross sensuality of his life. He may succeed, too, in his attempt to hide from the sight of man his guilt. Fig leaves may suffice to cover our sins from human eyes, but in the presence of the Almighty who knoweth all things, how empty and shallow are those attempts! It takes something more than man-made aprons, good works, generous deeds, to hide away sin.

Somewhere in the garden of Eden the Lord God slew the first sacrificial victim, an innocent animal that had nothing to do with the transgression of the guilty pair. Somewhere in the paradise of Eden the ground drank the blood of the first offering for sin, and from that harmless and blameless creature a coat was made to cover up the shame and the nakedness of the man and his wife. It is a picture of the covering, the atonement, the washing away of our sins in the sacrificial victim on the cross of Calvary.

The chapter ends with this final word:

> And the Lord God said, Behold, the man is become as one of us, to know good and evil: and now, lest he put forth his hand, and take also of the tree of life, and eat, and live forever: therefore the Lord God sent him forth from the garden of Eden, to till the ground from whence he was taken. So he drove out the man; and he placed at the east of the garden of Eden cherubims, and a flaming sword which turned every way, to keep the way of the tree of life.

What could that mean? The tree of life is taken from the man "lest he put forth his hand, and eat, and live forever." It means that had the man in his sin eaten of the tree of life, he would have lived forever in his sin, in his wretchedness and misery. He would have been confirmed in his sin; and confirmation in sin is eternal hell. He would have lived forever in a body of death, a frail body that is forever perishing, subject to all the ills and hurts that flesh is heir to. Death is given to man as a privilege and a release, that he might die to this life of sin and live to God forever. Revelation 9:6 describes the torment and horror of men who seek death and cannot find it. "And in those days shall men seek death, and shall not find it, and shall desire to die, and death shall flee from them." Death was a merciful provision on the part of the Lord God, and any man who lives long enough will come to recognize in the summons of the pale horseman a release from bodily affliction that ultimately grows unendurable.

One time a dear friend of mine asked me to lead a revival meeting in his church. I gladly accepted the invitation and was a guest in his home for the duration of the campaign. During those days I learned of a great sorrow that had broken the hearts of the couple. Their only son, a boy of thirteen years, became desperately ill of a dreadful disease. The lad suffered untold agonies as his body was torn with convulsions. Then the day came that the boy died. I asked my friend, "Didn't it nearly tear your heart out when the day came for the boy to die?"

"No," replied my pastor friend. "No, it was not that way at all. Our boy was so sick, suffering so intensely that I went down on my knees by his bed and prayed to God that, if it could be His will, He would not let him suffer any longer. I prayed God to take him to heaven, to let him be released; his suffering was too great. And when our boy died a great burden was lifted from our hearts because of his merciful release."

It is thus that death comes to man, that the tree of life has been removed from our grasp, "lest we eat, and live forever," live forever in this frail body of pain and sorrow.

There is a way back to God, back to the tree of life, back to the paradise of God our Saviour. "And . . . [the Lord God] placed at the east of the garden of Eden cherubims." In every instance where the cherubims are mentioned, they are connected with, and are symbols of, the divine mercy and grace. They are not ministers of vengeance; they are not messengers of judgment. In the holy of holies was the ark of the covenant. On the top of the ark of the covenant was the mercy seat. On each side of the mercy seat were the cherubims, their eyes full upon it, their wings covering it. Between them flamed the Shekinah, the fire of the glory and the presence of God. To that altar came the high priest, with blood of atonement, and there the mercy and forgiveness of the Holy One met the repentance and confession of man.

It was so on the east side of the garden of Eden after the man had been driven out. The man who was rebellious and self-willed in the garden of Eden was invited back, in repentance and faith, to bow, to worship, to come home, to find peace, to seek forgiveness and shelter at the altar of the mercy of God. The cherubims are there, symbols of the divine love and grace. The Shekinah glory is there, the pointed, lambent flame that keeps open the way to the tree of life. The altar of God is there, the place of prayer and of worship. And God himself is there, ready to receive the humble penitent in mercy and forgiveness.

O my friend, will you not come to Him now?

> Come, ye sinners, poor and needy,
> Weak and wounded, sick and sore;
> Jesus ready stands to save you,
> Full of pity, love, and power.

Let the deepest answer of our hearts be,

> I will arise and go to Jesus,
> He will embrace me in His arms,
> In the arms of my dear Saviour,
> Oh, there are ten thousand charms.

It is the gospel of the grace of the Son of God. Here it is in the first part of the first book of the Bible—the "protevangelium," the first announcement. The grace of God is freely and fully given to all who come to Him with humble and contrite hearts.

8
The Night of the Passover

(Ex. 12:12-13)

> For I will pass through the land of Egypt this night, and will smite
> all the firstborn in the land of Egypt, both man and beast; and against
> all the gods of Egypt I will execute judgment: I am the Lord.
>
> And the blood shall be to you a token upon the houses where ye
> are: and when I see the blood, I will pass over you, and the plague
> shall not be upon you to destroy you, when I smite the land of Egypt
> (Ex. 12:12-13).

The twelfth chapter of Exodus is, perhaps, the most solemn and serious of all chapters in the Old Testament. It records the institution of the memorial of the Passover. The importance of the memorial is evidenced in the fact that the sacrifice inaugurates a new calendar. "And the Lord spake unto Moses and Aaron in the land of Egypt, saying, This month shall be unto you the beginning of months: it shall be the first month of the year to you." It is to be the beginning of a new life for the people of God. They begin their pilgrimage to the Promised Land this very month, on the middle day of this month, and that means that the day is sacred and hallowed forever. It marks the new departure, when slavery ceases and life really begins.

The world, however, finds something strange about this. The world thinks just the opposite to what God says in His Book, for, to the world, becoming a Christian and beginning the heavenly pilgrimage is not the commencement of life but the end of life. To many the beginning of the Christian life means the end of any real joy, the termination of all genuine pleasure. To them there is nothing glorious to celebrate in the giving up of the fleshpots of Egypt; to them there is no cause to change the calendar when the Christian life commences. The good times are in Egypt; the doleful, drab, colorless, uninteresting times lie ahead down the Christian road. God, however, avows just the opposite; and the true experience of any Christian pilgrim will corroborate the Word of the Lord. It is the old life around the fleshpots of Egypt that is slavery and bondage; it is the new life in Christ that is full to the brim, glorious, and running over. So the Lord informs Moses and Aaron of the inauguration of the new calendar. It is to be the first month of a new year, a new life, a new devotion, a new way, and this day of the Passover is to be a memorial forever.

It is remarkable how God ordained the memorial to be observed. He placed it among families. "Speak," said God, "to the congregation of Israel, and say that each family, each head of the house is to take every man a lamb according to the house of their fathers, a lamb for a house." This memorial is not to be kept in solitude. A man is not to observe it by himself, but he is to partake of it in the orbit of a home, a family. God has ordained that the family unit is primary and fundamental. God builds the nations by units of families. God strengthens His churches by family ties and home religion. The memorial of the Passover, the services of the church, are not for father alone, nor for mother alone, nor for the children alone, but for the entire household. The father and the mother in the home are charged with the responsibility of teaching the children. "And it shall come to pass," said the Lord God, "when your children shall say unto you, What mean ye by this service? that ye shall say, It is the sacrifice of the Lord's passover, who passed over the houses of the children of Israel in Egypt, when he smote the Egyptians, and delivered our houses" (Ex. 12:26-27). God intended that true religion everlastingly be a family religion, shared by father, mother, son, daughter, and the entire household.

The Death Angel

The night following the fourteenth day of Nisan was a dark, terrible night. The Lord Almighty passed judgment, not only upon Egypt, but upon Israel also. Heretofore God had shown that a tremendous difference existed between Israel and Egypt. Through all the admonitory, preliminary plagues the children of Jacob were untouched. They enjoyed a painless, unbought exemption. The murrain had not destroyed their cattle, the hail and the locusts had not ruined their fields, the darkness had not obscured their villages. While the Egyptians reeled under the thunderbolts of God's wrath, the Israelites basked in the sunlight of His protection. The judgment and the visitation of God on that awful night were to be on all alike— Egyptian, Israelite, stranger, sojourner—everyone.

From a close study of God's Word, it seems that in the final analysis the judgments of God, the demands of the Almighty, are never mitigated by the extenuating factors of birth, ancestry, genealogy, race, nation. The fearless preaching of John the Baptist was just that.

> But when he saw many of the Pharisees and Sadducees come to his baptism, he said unto them, O generation of vipers, who hath warned you to flee from the wrath to come? Bring forth therefore fruits meet for repentance: and think not to say within yourselves, We have Abraham to our father: for I say unto you, that God is able of these stones to raise up children unto Abraham (Matt. 3:7-9).

John the Baptist is here denying special privilege and favoritism before God. In God's presence we stand all alike—condemned sinners, saved only from the wrath to come by repenting of our sins and by casting ourselves upon the mercy of God. Lineage has nothing to do with it. Just like the night of the Passover: all alike trembled before the black terror, listening for the rustling of the awful wings. The heart of each one beat faster as he hid himself behind the sprinkled blood. Oh, that tense moment when the destroying angel scrutinized the lintels and doorposts of the homes of the people! The land of Goshen, as well as the land of Egypt, faced death. This is the great argument of the first chapters of the book of Romans: "For there is no respect of persons with God. For as many as have sinned without law shall also perish without law: and as many as have sinned in the law shall be judged by the law" (Rom. 2:11-12).

> Are we better than they? No, in no wise: for we have before proved both Jews and Gentiles, that they are all under sin; as it is written,

There is none righteous, no, not one. . . . For all have sinned, and come short of the glory of God (Romans 3:9-10, 23).

By birth we do not inherit an exemption from the judgment of death; no, not even if we are children of Abraham. All who sin are under the condemnation of sin, face the penalty of sin. Whether Egyptian or Israelite, all are under the eyes of the death that is. The destroying angel will visit us all.

The Way of Salvation

Who, then, can be saved? God is good, but the goodness of God will not pronounce a sinner safe until he follows the way of escape. The goodness of God will not save him, but it will point out and provide for a salvation that is as sure and steadfast as the eternal throne of the Almighty. What the child of Abraham could not possess by birth he might obtain by grace. And if an Egyptian so chose to heed the appeal of God, he also might have the gift of life. God's way of salvation is the same for all men. It is the way of blood, the way of atonement, the way of substitution, the way of the cross.

During those awful days of judgment the people were to choose a lamb without blemish and keep it four days until it became, as it were, a member of the household, loved as a part of the family. It was then to be solemnly slain by the head of the house as their representative, in their stead. The blood of the substitutionary lamb was then to be sprinkled on the doorposts of the house and on the lintels above. The act was an open confession, publicly exhibited, that they stood in peril before the destroying angel. This was blood of expiation, the washing away of guilt by suffering, atonement. A life had been sacrificed, the penalty of guilt had been suffered; death, the wages of sin, had been paid. "When I see the blood, I will pass over you." Nothing more was required. The debt had been covered in full.

In the memorial of the Passover, which the Jewish people were to keep sacred forever, there was to be firmly fixed in their hearts always the remembrance that the lamb was slain in their stead, for them, a substitutionary sacrifice. In commemoration of the mighty deliverance, every first-born was to be set aside for the Lord. "Thou shalt set apart unto the Lord all that openeth the matrix, and every firstling that cometh of a beast which thou hast; the males shall be the Lord's" (Ex. 13:12).

But what was to be done with the first-born of an unclean animal? It was to be slain or it was to be redeemed by the sacrifice of a lamb. "And every firstling of an ass thou shalt redeem with a lamb; and if thou wilt not redeem it, then thou shalt break his neck: and all the first-born of man among thy children shalt thou redeem" (Ex. 13:13). In the Old Testament all living things were classed as clean or unclean. Man is in the latter class—he is unclean. He has sin in his heart, lust in his soul, evil in every imagination. Unredeemed, unregenerated in his natural, fallen state, he is born to die. He is worthless. Like the firstling of an ass whose neck must otherwise be broken, he must also be redeemed. He must die or someone must die for him. It is one or the other, the terrible alternative forced upon God and God's moral world by our sins. If the manchild is to live, the lamb must be slain as a substitutionary sacrifice and the blood poured out as an offering of expiation and atonement. No Hebrew could ever forget the solemnity of the meaning of that Passover memorial and the redemption with the sacrifice of a lamb that bought back the forfeited life of his first-born.

The Lamb of God, Our Savior

The Passover is a gospel before the gospel. In 1 Corinthians 5:7, Paul says, "Christ our passover is sacrificed for us." All those colorful, dramatic ordinances and rituals of the Old Testament prefigured and foreshadowed the work of Christ. Redemption, substitution, atonement, are no afterthought of God. The cross was not a "happen-so" in history. The whole sacrificial system of Judaism had as its highest purpose to adumbrate the coming of the wonderful Savior whose blood could wash away our sins: "Forasmuch as ye know that ye were not redeemed with corruptible things, . . . but with the precious blood of Christ, as of a lamb without blemish and without spot: who verily was foreordained before the foundation of the world, but was manifest in these last times for you" (1 Pet. 1:18-20).

Among all these memorials and ordinances and rituals that set forth in the Old Testament the work of the coming Savior, none is fraught with more meaning than the ordinance of the Passover. Three things regarding our hope in Christ Jesus are gloriously and eloquently prefigured here.

First, our redemption and deliverance are procured in the death of the Lamb. It is the cross that opens the flood-gates of love and pardon. The life of Christ Jesus is beautiful and good beyond compare, but we are not saved by this beautiful life. We are saved by His death, by His atoning, sacrificial death. Christ Jesus was without fault: "I find in him no fault at all," said Pilate. But "without the shedding of blood there is no remission" of sins. His precious and obedient life is not the procuring cause of our salvation; it is His death on the cross. If to this hour He had remained, going through the cities of the world "doing good," we would yet be in our sins. The veil of the Temple would still be unrent, barring the approach of the worshiper to God. It was His death that rent the mystic curtain from top to bottom. Through the blood of the Lamb we may boldly approach the throne of grace, with no temple, no priest, no commandment to intervene.

> For this cause he is the mediator of the new testament, that by means of death, for the redemption of the transgressions that were under the first testament, they which are called might receive the promise of eternal inheritance. . . . Having therefore, brethren, boldness to enter into the holiest by the blood of Jesus, by a new and living way, which he hath consecrated for us, through the veil, that is to say, his flesh; . . . let us draw near with a true heart in full assurance of faith (Heb. 9:15; 10:19-22).

All these incomparably rich gifts that pertain to our salvation here in this world and in the world to come are poured out upon us through the death of Christ Jesus.

> Verily, verily, I say unto you, Except a corn of wheat fall into the ground and die, it abideth alone: but if it die, it bringeth forth much

fruit. . . . And I, if I be lifted up from the earth, will draw all men unto
me. This he said, signifying what death he should die (John 12: 24,
32-33).

He is that precious "corn of wheat" that is to be planted in the heart
of the earth. Even though He was the incarnate Son of God, yet He
would have remained alone had He not by death removed everything that prevents the union of His people with Him in the resurrection. He tasted death for every man that He might bring many
sons to glory. It is by His stripes, not by His obedient life, that we are
healed. It is on the cross that He bore our sins: "Who his own self
bare our sins in his own body on the tree, that we, being dead to
sins, should live unto righteousness: by whose stripes ye were
healed" (1 Pet. 2:24). Our salvation is rooted and grounded in the
blood of the atonement on the cross. "When I see the blood, I will
pass over you."

A second gospel message adumbrated in the ordinance of the
Passover, wonderfully fulfilled in Christ, is this: The atonement is
full and final, adequate and complete, the sure and sufficient
ground of our security and peace. Our redemption is a finished
work of grace, procured in the atoning blood of Christ. We do not
work for it, we do not inherit it; it is a gift of God. Nothing more is
required. Nothing can be added to it. The atonement for our sins is
forever and finally complete.

> Could my tears forever flow,
> Could my zeal no languor know,
> These for sin could not atone;
> Thou must save, and Thou alone:
> In my hand no price I bring,
> Simply to Thy cross I cling.

All God's claims and all Israel's needs were met in the blood of the
Passover lamb. Death might work outside, but under the blood
there were security and rest. The security we possess in Christ Jesus
does not depend upon us but upon His finished work. His work for
us is eternally and absolutely complete. Christ bowed His knees in
prayer and said to the Father, "I have finished the work which thou

gavest me to do" (John 17:4). Christ bowed His head on the cross and said, "It is finished" (John 19:30). What did He mean? He meant that the atoning sacrifice for our sins had been made; that the full price of our redemption had been paid. The work of the Holy Spirit *in* us may be multiplied a thousand times and added to each day, but the work of Christ *for* us is forever complete. In the shedding of blood is the remission of sins. In His sacrifice, in His blood, in His atoning grace, we are secure forever. On the cross He tasted death for every man. The threat of the angel of death holds no fear for the child of faith. "When I see the blood, I will pass over you."

The third gospel message prefigured to us in the memorial of the Passover concerns our response to the provisions of grace offered us by our loving Lord. The merits of the atoning blood are mediated to us through our personal acceptance of them. They are ours forever through simple faith, trust, obedience.

Had any son of Abraham despised the provisions of safety, he would have been partaker of the plague. Death would have entered his home. On the other hand, had any Egyptian trusted in the word of the Lord, accepted the way of deliverance, and sprinkled the blood on the doorposts of his home, he would have been saved. The difference between the Egyptians and the Israelites that dark night of judgment was not that Israel was fair and comely while the Egyptians were offensive and unattractive. No, if there was any difference that night of judgment and death, it lay in the spirit of acceptance or rejection of the mercies of God. The angel passing over looked for the faith and obedience that hid the soul behind the blood. The difference lay alone in the sprinkling of the blood.

The saved were those who publicly set apart their homes. The blood was openly exhibited. It was an unashamed act of faith. Suppose an Israelite had said: "I refuse to be a dupe of such bloody theology. Back in Abel's time they might have offered blood sacrifices, but in this modern day we have outgrown such heathenish notions. Are we not learned in all the arts and sciences of the Egyptians? Such a foolish thing as to think that the blood of a lamb could keep a soul from death! There shall be no blood sprinkled on my doorpost. This is a house of science and knowledge, not of supersti-

tion and fear." Then what would have happened? The darkness of
that dark night would have doubly fallen upon that house. Pride
would have turned to mourning, knowledge to tears and lamenta-
tion.

Or suppose an Israelite had said: "I may sprinkle the blood inside
the house where no one can see, or back of the house where no one
will know, but I positively refuse to strike the hyssop on the doorposts and lintels. I want my house to look like all the other houses of
the Egyptians, not separated from them." What would have happened? The Lord had said that the blood was to be openly dis-
played, where the world might see and know. But here is an Israelite
that is ashamed of the faith, of the way God has provided for his
salvation. What of that man? In his refusal and disobedience he is
lost. The angel of judgment and of death shall look for the blood on
the doorposts and lintels and shall not find it. Nothing stands between that soul and hell.

It is thus with the way of the Christian faith. We are openly, publicly, unashamedly to avow our trust in Christ's atoning blood. Our
salvation calls for an open stand for Christ, whatever the cost. "If
thou shalt confess with thy mouth the Lord Jesus, and shalt believe
in thine heart that God hath raised him from the dead, thou shalt be
saved. For with the heart man believeth unto righteousness, and
with the mouth confession is made unto salvation" (Rom. 10:9-10).
Our blessed Master said the same thing in another way. "Whosoever therefore shall confess me before men, him will I confess also
before my Father which is in heaven. But whosoever shall deny me
before men, him will I also deny before my father which is in
heaven" (Matt. 10:32-33). "Whosoever therefore shall be ashamed of
me and of my words in this adulterous and sinful generation; of him
also shall the Son of man be ashamed, when he cometh in the glory
of his Father with the holy angels" (Mark 8:38).

To be a secret disciple of Christ is an impossible thing. To be
ashamed of Christ is to be unworthy of Him. To refuse to confess
Him is to deny Him. To deny Him is to be lost. If we love Him and
trust in Him, we must openly, take our stand by His side, "tenting at
the cross." As the sprinkling of the blood of the Passover lamb was

on the doorposts, on the lintels, on the front of the houses, where all the world could know, so our faith in Christ must be open, public, where all the world can see. And as the public display of that sprinkled blood secured salvation for the sojourner in Egypt that dark night of death, so will a public avowal of faith and trust in the blood of the Lamb bring eternal life to the believer in the day of the wrath and the judgment of Almighty God. "And one of the elders answered, saying unto me, What are these which are arrayed in white robes? and whence came they? And I said unto him, Sir, thou knowest. And he said unto me, These are they which came out of great tribulation, and have washed their robes, and made them white in the blood of the Lamb" (Rev. 7:13-14).

9
Types of Calvary
(Luke 24:25-27,44-46)

Then he said unto them, O fools, and slow of heart to believe all that the prophets have spoken:

Ought not Christ to have suffered these things, and to enter into his glory?

And beginning at Moses and all the prophets, he expounded unto them in all the scriptures the things concerning himself.

And he said unto them, These are the words which I spake unto you, while I was yet with you, that all things must be fulfilled, which were written in the law of Moses, and in the prophets, and in the psalms, concerning me.

Then opened he their understanding, that they might understand the scriptures,

And said unto them, Thus it is written, and thus it behoved Christ to suffer, and to rise from the dead the third day (Luke 24:25-27,44-46).

In our text we see the marvelous unfolding of the Word of God that Jesus laid before the two disciples on the way to Emmaus. In the latter part of the chapter the Lord opened the minds of the eleven disciples that they might understand the Scriptures. The Scripture expressly says that "beginning at Moses and all the prophets" (and then in the latter part of the chapter of our text, taking the three categories into which the Old Testament is divided—the law, the prophets, and the holy writings—through all of these divisions), the Lord showed them all things concerning himself. That meant that what we read in the Old Testament are types, pictures, outlines, and presentations of the great truth that God would have us learn in Christ Jesus.

One of the most profitable and spiritually rewarding of all the studies by which one could open his heart to the truth of the Word of God is the study of the types of the Lord in the Old Testament. This is a type: "And as Moses lifted up the serpent in the wilderness, even so must the Son of man be lifted up: That whosoever believeth in him should not perish, but have eternal life" (John 3:14-15).

Why should God have told Moses to take a serpent cast in brass and to lift it up in the midst of the camp? If someone was dying, having been bitten by a little tenuous serpent, he would live if he would look at the brass replica. God was teaching, training, and getting us ready for the great spiritual truth of our salvation in Christ Jesus. Why should the Lord say to Israel (and here is another type): "Tonight the angel of death will visit all the homes in the land of Egypt. But if there is a home that will take the blood of a lamb and sprinkle it in the form of a cross on the lintel and the doorpost on either side, the angel of death will pass over you." To those who were under the blood there was life and salvation, not death and judgment.

That is a type. God did that to teach us what Christ means to us. The purpose of the whole sacrificial system was that we might learn the nomenclature of heaven, that we might understand what God meant when he spoke of an "altar," a "sacrifice," "a propitiatory," an "atonement." The Lord was teaching us what happened when Christ came into the world.

The First Type in the Old Testament

We shall look at the first type and the last type which lay open to view the great spiritual truth of the atoning grace of God in Christ Jesus. The first type in the Bible was:

> And the Lord God caused a deep sleep to fall upon Adam, and he slept: and he took one of his ribs [side], and closed up the flesh instead thereof; And the rib, which the Lord God had taken from man [bana, "built," as one would build the temple] made he a woman, and brought her unto the man. And Adam said, This is now bone of my

bones, and flesh of my flesh: she shall be called [Isha], Woman because she was taken out of [Ish], Man. Therefore shall a man leave his
father and his mother, and shall cleave unto his wife: and they shall be
one flesh (Gen. 2:21-24).

Let us look now at the New Testament discussion of that type. The
apostle Paul had pertinent comments on this subject.

In Ephesians 5 Paul spoke of the church: "Christ also loved the
church, and gave Himself for it" (Eph. 5:25). In the thirtieth verse he
said, "For we are members of his body, of his flesh, and of his
bones" (Eph. 5:30). Remember the type, "And Adam said, this is
now bone of my bones and flesh of my flesh." The fulfillment of that
type is that we are members of his body, of his flesh, and of his
bones. Genesis says, "Therefore shall a man leave his father and his
mother, and shall cleave unto his wife: and they shall be one flesh."
Ephesians says: "For this cause shall a man leave his father and his
mother, and shall be joined unto his wife, and they two shall be one
flesh.

"This is a great [musterion] mystery: but I speak concerning
Christ and the church" (Eph. 5:31-32). Paul was very clear about his
comparison.

Paul said, "But I speak concerning Christ and the church." This is
a type of what God is teaching us in the relationship between Christ
and his church. As Eve was taken out of the heart of Adam, from his
side, so the church is taken and born out of the riven side of our
Lord. We are born in his tears, in his agony, in his cross, in his suffering, in his blood, and in his death.

The Last Type in the Old Testament

The last type in the Old Testament, described and fulfilled in the
New Testament, is: "Jesus, when he had cried again with a loud
voice, yielded up the ghost, And, behold, the veil of the temple was
rent in twain from the top to the bottom" (Matt. 27:50-51).

How meticulously does God stay true to his type! The veil was
torn not from the bottom to the top as though men had torn it apart,
which is as men would tear it, but from the top to the bottom. It is
doubtful that even the strength of men could have torn it, for Jo-

sephus says that horses could not have rent that thick and heavy and woven veil. "Behold, the veil of the temple was rent in twain from the top to the bottom; and the earth did quake, and the rocks rent" (Matt. 27:51). The type was made possible in the Old Testament when the Lord God said to Moses: "Thou shalt rear up the tabernacle according to the fashion thereof which was shewed thee in the mount" (Ex. 26:30). Just exactly as God said to do it, so Moses did.

Often I avow that God's people ought to obey the instructions of the Lord just exactly as God has said to. An illustration can be found in our baptismal service. I did not invent the baptismal ordinance. This church did not originate it. John the Baptist said that he was given the form of baptism from God himself. When God revealed its meaning, we learned that baptism means the burial and the resurrection of our Lord, our death with him and our resurrection to a new life in Christ. It is a glorious picture, a promise, a harbinger, and a type of our ultimate, victorious resurrection. We are to baptize as God has shown us.

God's instructions for the creation of the veil were most explicit:

> And thou shalt make a veil of blue, and purple, and scarlet, and fine twined linen of cunning work: with cherubims shall it be made: And thou shalt hang it upon four pillars of shittim wood overlaid with gold: their hooks shall be of gold, upon the four sockets of silver. And thou shalt hang up the veil under the taches [the clasps], that thou mayest bring in thither within the veil the ark of the testimony: and the veil shall divide unto you between the holy place and the most holy (Ex. 26:31-33).

This is God's pattern that he showed Moses from heaven.

Now let us look at the use of the type. In the book of Hebrews we read:

> Having therefore, brethren, boldness to enter into the holiest by the blood of Jesus, By a new and living way, which he hath consecrated for us, through the veil, that is to say, his flesh; And having an high priest over the house of God; Let us draw near with a true heart in full assurance of faith. (Heb. 10:19-22).

The author of Hebrews used that veil as a type, and this is the last type used in the Bible. The veil is a type of the flesh of our Lord, the incarnation of our Lord. The glory of the presence of God was veiled with the flesh of Jesus Christ. He was deity, God—and God incarnate, veiled in flesh.

Once in a while one would see the glory of God shining through the physical frame of our Lord, as on the top of the mount of transfiguration. For just a moment, even through the veil of his flesh, the glory of God shone through and the three apostles saw it. No wonder Peter said, "Let us stay here!" It was a glory of glories, seeing God in the flesh. But for the most part, his glory was veiled and the Lord's flesh covered the deity, the shining iridescence, the presence of God. If one had looked upon the Lord, he would have seen a man like other men, made as his brethren. But he was God in the flesh, and the flesh veiled his deity.

It is in the tearing of the veil that we have access into the very presence of the Almighty. As long as the veil was there, as long as Christ was in the flesh, as long as our Lord did not die, we were shut out from God. It is in the tearing of the veil, in the rending of the veil that we have access into the presence of God. Had the Lord remained in his flesh all of his years and had continued to go through all the cities of Israel doing good, to this present day we would still be in our sins. Not by his holy, beautiful, heavenly, celestial, righteous, and perfect life are we saved. It is by his stripes that we are healed.

However beautiful, perfect, and holy the life of Christ may have been; however the veil may have been of blue, purple, and scarlet with inwoven cherubim in the fine twined linen—as long as that veil was there, it shut us out from God. But since the veil was torn, we have had access into the holy of holies. So it is with our blessed Lord. It is in his death, in the rending of the veil that we have boldness to enter into the holy of holies by the blood, the death, the sacrifice of Jesus. Let us then draw near with a true heart in full assurance of faith. Jesus has opened the way in his death in the rending of the veil. He has made an entrance for us into glory. That is the type.

The author of the Hebrews used the type in one other way, one of the most precious of all the interpretations of a type that one could find in God's Book. He spoke of God's promises to us, emphasizing the faithfulness of God. He wrote:

> Wherein God, willing more abundantly to shew unto the heirs of promise the immutability of his counsel, confirmed it by an oath: That by two immutable things, in which it was impossible for God to lie, we might have a strong consolation, who have fled for refuge to lay hold upon the hope set before us: Which hope we have as an anchor of the soul, both sure and stedfast, and which *entereth into that within the veil;* Whither the forerunner is for us entered, even Jesus, made an high priest for ever after the order of Melchisidec (Heb. 6:17-20).

This type is this: When the veil was torn apart our forerunner, our Lord Jesus, entered in. In his death did he become glorified and immortalized. He entered into glory. Our hope is in that same Lord Jesus, the anchor of the soul, who entered into the veil, beyond the veil, and through the veil. For the Lord made a way for us, and we follow with him into glory.

Ah, what God hath done for us! He has taught us these precious and blessed assurances in the meaning of the death of Christ. God pictured it so that when Christ died, we might understand what he was doing. Oh, the grace, love, and provision for the saving of our souls and the gathering of his chosen, redeemed people into that upper and better world that is yet to come!

10
The Remission of Sins

(Luke 24:44-53)

And he said unto them, These are the words which I spake unto you, while I was yet with you, that all things must be fulfilled, which were written in the law of Moses, and in the prophets, and in the psalms, concerning me.

Then opened he their understanding, that they might understand the scriptures,

And said unto them, Thus it is written, and thus is behoved Christ to suffer, and to rise from the dead the third day:

And that repentance and remission of sins should be preached in his name among all nations, beginning at Jerusalem.

And ye are witnesses of these things.

And, behold, I send the promise of my Father upon you: but tarry ye in the city of Jerusalem, until ye be endued with power from on high.

And he led them out as far as to Bethany, and he lifted up his hands, and blessed them.

And it came to pass, while he blessed them, he was parted from them, and carried up into heaven.

And they worshipped him, and returned to Jerusalem with great joy:

And were continually in the temple, praising and blessing God. Amen (Luke 24:44-53).

The text of the message is: "And he said unto them, Thus it is written, and thus it behooved Christ to suffer, and to rise from the dead the third day: And that repentance and remission of sins should be preached in his name among all nations" (Luke 24:46-47).

This is the gospel; this is our assignment; this is the duty and responsibility of a true preacher of Jesus; and this is the truth held inviolate by the New Testament church. What is our duty, our mandate? It is this: Because Christ suffered for our sins and was raised for our justification, we are to preach the remission of sins to all the nations.

If I am correct in my appraisal, the modern church, as one sees it in the world, proliferated through many denominations, is giving itself to a thousand other interests and enterprises. I do not deny that there are political repercussions in preaching the gospel. I would be the last to say that there are not social ameliorations and reforms that are inherent in the Word of God. I do not contradict the feeling that there are cultural overtones and concomitants that attend the preaching of the message of Christ. But I do avow by the authority of the Lord Himself and the Word He spelled out plainly and clearly that our assignment and task is to preach the gospel of the remission of sins.

What is the gospel? Jesus defined it as His death, His suffering and burial, and, on the third day, His resurrection from the dead. On the basis of that atonement and that triumph over sin, death, and the grave, we are to preach the forgiveness of sins. This is also spelled out plainly by the apostle Paul:

> Moreover, brethren, I declare unto you the gospel which I preached unto you, which also ye have received, and wherein ye stand; By which also ye are saved, if ye keep in memory what I preached unto you, unless ye have believed in vain. For I delivered unto you first of all that which I also received, how that Christ died for our sins according to the scriptures; And that he was buried, and that he rose again the third day according to the scriptures (1 Cor. 15:1-4).

It is possible to address the energies of the church to all of the problems of society—economic, political, social, and cultural. But when the gospel message in the Bible is declared, it addresses itself to the human heart, to the individual soul. Have you been saved? Are your sins forgiven?

The gospel message of Christ addresses the heart. To put new clothes on a man does not make him a new man. To educate a man does not make him a new man. Giving him all of the fine cultural amenities to observe in life will not change his character. The gospel message addresses itself to the man in his soul, in his heart—at the fountain source of his life. It seeks to create in the man a new being. This is the gospel message according to the Word of the Lord.

The Curse of the World

The gospel message, according to our Savior, concerns His death for our sins on the cross and His resurrection from the grave for our justification. The gospel message addressed to the human heart concerns itself with the remission of sin. When I hold the Book in my hand and turn through its pages, I find that the whole Bible has to do with sin. The scene opens in the Garden of Eden when the Lord said to our first parents, "In the day that thou eatest thereof thou shalt surely die" (Gen. 2:17). This is the curse of the world.

If one sins against a friend, something dies within him. If one sins against a partner, something will die between them. If one sins against his home, something will die in it. If one sins against himself, something will die in him. When one sins against God, something dies between him and the Lord. When sin is added to anything—to any gift, any virtue, any achievement—it will spell grief and misery and death. A gun plus sin will produce violence and murder. Success plus sin will produce egotism, pride, and overbearing ostentation. Money plus sin will produce greed, bribery, and blackmail. Love plus sin turns to lust. A home plus sin will produce an atmosphere like hell.

Alcohol plus sin—a car plus sin—any gift of God plus sin is damned to misery and perdition. God said, "In the day that thou eatest thereof thou shalt surely die." There is a curse in sin.

The Everlasting Stain of Sin

There is an everlasting stain about sin. Sin is in your soul, in your memory, in your heart, in your life, and piece and parcel with you. Sin carries with it an everlasting stain.

In Genesis 49:1 Jacob called his sons and said, "Gather yourself together that I may tell you that which shall befall you in the last days." One of those sons was to receive the blessing. He was to be the one through whom the Messiah was to come. So he turned to his firstborn son. The blessing should have been given to Reuben, but the patriarch said:

> Reuben, thou art my firstborn, my might, and the beginning of my strength, the excellency of dignity, and the excellency of power. Unstable as water, thou shalt not excel; because thou wentest up to thy father's bed; then defiledst thou it: he went up to my couch (Gen. 49:3-4).

As Reuben stood there that day at the head of the twelve patriarchal sons of Jacob, he drew himself up to his full height. He was the firstborn; surely the blessing would be his. But Jacob pointed out to him a secret sin that he thought had been forgotten and buried; and it was as livid, as vivid, and as scarlet that day when Jacob looked upon him as on the day when he committed it. Your sins will be that way when you stand before the judgment bar of Almighty God. They were committed in youth, in childhood, in the dark, in secret; but they will be as vivid and livid in the day of judgment as they were the day when you committed them.

If Reuben did not receive the blessing, then the second son, Simeon, should have received it. If he did not, then the third son, Levi, should. Jacob turned to them and said: "Simeon and Levi are brethren; instruments of cruelty are in their habitations. O my soul, come not thou into their secret" (Gen. 49:5-6).

What Jacob was referring to is recorded in the Bible and had happened over forty years before. It was a murderous and bloody sin that the two brothers had committed. I would think that Simeon and Levi, as they stood there, thought that what they committed forty years ago had been buried and forgotten in the passing of time. But in the great hour of judgment their sin, too, was as vivid, as livid, and as crimson as the day that they committed it. We do not get beyond the everlasting stain of sin in human life.

The Guilt of Us All

Sin is the common denominator of us all. It is the guilt of us all. The best man in the Old Testament, Job, cried, saying: "I have sinned; what shall I do unto thee, O thou preserver of men?" (Job 7:20). Vice is against society. Crime is against law and order. Sin is against God. That is why in Psalm 51:4 David said, "Against thee, thee only, have I sinned, and done this evil in thy sight." We only sin against God. We violate law. We scorn the law. We disobey all of the perogatives and mandates of men. But sin is against God and God alone.

No need to say to me, "Do not sin." I have sinned. To lecture me about it, to speak to me about it, to ask a reform concerning it has no pertinency whatsoever. I have already sinned.

One time I was driving down a road when a man in a new, flashy, big car passed me rapidly. After a little while I came to a place where the road made a direct right-angle turn. When I got to that turn I stopped the car, for the man in that big automobile, going so rapidly, had been unable to negotiate the sharp turn. On the other side was a bank about waist high. He had driven that car into the bank with a terrific impact.

There happened to be a farmhouse just beyond. When I arrived there I looked at the car. It was bloodsplattered. I looked at the man. The farmer and his wife were helping him into the farmhouse. He was badly hurt. There was no need to sit by the side of the man and say: "You ought not to drive fast. Didn't you know that?" The man was hurt and bleeding. Something needed to be done then. It is the same way with our sins.

What I want to know is, what is a message in a word for me when I have sinned? "What shall I do, O thou preserver of men, for I have sinned?" That is the address of the gospel. That is what the Bible is about. The stain in my soul and the sin in my life—is there a remission of sins of which somebody knows? Is there a way of salvation so that, even though I have sinned, I still might see the face of God?

The whole Bible has to do with the remission, the forgiveness of our sins. In the Garden of Eden the Bible tells of forgiveness of sins, beginning with a covering. The Lord slew an innocent animal and poured out its blood, and the earth drank it up. God took skins of an innocent animal which laid down its life to cover the nakedness of our first parents. In the Temple worship the mercy seat was sprinkled with the blood of expiation. The message of the prophets as in Isaiah is: "Come now, and let us reason together, saith the Lord: though your sins be as scarlet, they shall be white as snow; though they be red like crimson, they shall be as wool" (Isa. 1:18). "All we like sheep have gone astray; we have turned every one to his own way; and the Lord hath laid on him the iniquity of us all" (Isa. 53:6).

The ministry of the Lord Jesus is that He shall save His people from their sins. The Lord Himself came to give His life as a ransom for many. The blessed installation and introduction of the Lord's Supper is, "This is my blood of the new testament, which is shed for many for the remission of sins" (Matt. 26:28). It is the preaching of the apostle Peter. When the convicted people cried, "Men and brethren, what shall we do?" (Acts 2:37), the reply as recorded in the book of Acts is: "Repent, and be baptized every one of you in the name of Jesus Christ for [because of] the remission of sins" (Acts 2:38). John said, "And the blood of Jesus Christ his Son cleanseth us from all sin" (1 John 1:7). Paul said:

> For when we were yet without strength in due time Christ died for the ungodly. For scarcely for a righteous man will one die: yet peradventure for a good man some would even dare to die. But God commendeth his love toward us, in that, while we were yet sinners, Christ died for us (Rom. 5:6-8).

This is the glorious apocalyptic revelation: "Unto him that loved us, and washed us from our sins in his own blood, And hath made up kings and priests unto God and his Father; to him be glory and honor and dominion and power for ever and ever. Amen" (Rev. 1:5-6).

> What are these which are arrayed in white robes? and whence came they? And I said unto him, Sir, thou knowest. And he said to me, These are they which came out of great tribulation, and have washed

their robes, and made them white in the blood of the Lamb (Rev. 7:13-14).

The message from our Lord Himself is that Christ suffered and was raised from the dead and that remission of sins should be preached in His name to all people. That is the good news. That is the message. That is the gospel!

11
The Crimson Flow

(John 19:28-35)

After this, Jesus knowing that all things were now accomplished, that the scripture might be fulfilled, saith, I thirst.

Now there was set a vessel full of vinegar: and they filled a sponge with vinegar, and put it upon hyssop, and put it to his mouth.

When Jesus therefore had received the vinegar, he said, It is finished: and he bowed his head, and gave up the ghost.

The Jews therefore, because it was the preparation, that the bodies should not remain upon the cross on the sabbath day, (for that sabbath day was an high day,) besought Pilate that their legs might be broken, and that they might be taken away.

Then came the soldiers, and brake the legs of the first, and of the other which was crucified with him.

But when they came to Jesus, and saw that he was dead already, they brake not his legs:

But one of the soldiers with a spear pierced his side and forthwith came there out blood and water.

And he that saw it bare record, and his record is true: and he knoweth that he saith true, that ye might believe (John 19:28-35).

In 1 John 5 the beloved apostle again wrote of Jesus: "This is he that came by water and blood, even Jesus Christ; not by water only, but by water and blood. And there are three that bear witness in earth, the spirit, and the water, and the blood: and these three agree in one" (1 John 5:6,8). One cannot read these words without sensing something deeply spiritual in what John was describing.

The crucifixion of our Lord, of anyone, was a horrible thing. There has never been invented a death as agonizing and as tortuous as the Roman custom of crucifying traitors, criminals, and enemies of the empire. Usually when a man was crucified, he writhed in agony on the cross for a full two or three days. Crucifixion did not destroy in itself any vital organ, so the criminal just hung there until he finally died of exhaustion, which usually took about three days.

Our Lord did not die of exhaustion. He laid down His life and gave up His spirit. So soon did He die, in six hours, that when Pilate heard it he marvelled that Jesus was so soon dead and inquired officially of the centurion who presided over the execution to see whether or not Jesus had really expired in so short a time.

Crucifying enemies of the state was almost a daily occurrence, and the soldiers who carried out the crucifixions were brutal and cruel. They executed slaves, traitors, malefactors, and enemies; and they executed them everywhere and all the time. Such a diverse population as was conquered by the rule of Rome was accompanied by much restiveness, war, and oppression. Judaea was the most restive and rebellious of all. Crucifixion was a common experience, in Judaea and to see men hanging helplessly on crosses was a common sight. The soldiers were adept in murder, in crucifixion, and in execution. The Scriptures say that when they came to look at Jesus, they saw that he was already dead. These hardened men knew when a man was dead; and, looking at Jesus, they saw that he was already dead.

Blood and Water Flowed Mingled Down

To make absolutely sure that Jesus was dead, one of the soldiers took a spear and thrust it into his heart. When he pulled out the spear, out flowed blood and water. So impressive was the phenomenon that blood and water should have poured out of the wound created by the thrust of the spear that John paused to record it.

> The Jews therefore, because it was the preparation, that the bodies should not remain upon the cross on the sabbath day, (for that sabbath day was an high day,) besought Pilate that their legs might be broken, and that they might be taken away. Then came the soldiers, and brake the legs of the first, and of the other which was crucified with him. But when they came to Jesus, and saw that he was dead already, they brake not his legs: But one of the soldiers with a spear

pierced his side, and forthwith came there out blood and water. And he that saw it bare record, and his record is true: and he knoweth that he saith true, that ye might believe. For these things were done, that the scripture should be fulfilled, A bone of him shall not be broken. And again another scripture saith, They shall look on him whom they pierced (John 19:31-37).

What impressed John so deeply that he should write so emphatically about blood and water flowing from the wounds of our Lord? One must look at what John was doing and how he did it to thus see what he meant by his emphasis of blood and water pouring out of the open side of our Lord.

Jesus Taught the People with Signs

When John wrote his Gospel he never used the word *miracle*. There are two words that are constantly used for miracle in the New Testament, especially to describe the marvelous works of our Lord. One is *tera*; that is, "miracle" in the sense of a wonder, "a great amazement," something that had never been seen before. "It was never so seen in Israel" (Matt. 9:33), cried the disciples and the people as they looked at the *tera*, the "wonder" of the works of the Lord. John never used the word *tera*.

Another word for "miracle" is *dunamis*—that is, miracle in the sense of a great manifestation of the power of God that God is able to do such a thing. John likewise never used the word *dunamis*, but he used another word all through his Gospel. He uses the word *semeion*, "sign." What he meant is this. Not only were there spiritual truth and revelation in what Jesus was saying as He taught the people; but there was no less truth, spiritual revelation, in what Jesus did. What He did was a *semeion*, a "sign" that pointed to the truth of God.

The Revelation begins, "The Revelation of Jesus Christ, which God gave unto him, to shew unto his servants things which must shortly come to pass; and he sent and signified it by his angel unto his servant John" (Rev. 1:1). If one pronounced the word *signified* "sign-ified," it would mean more. "He 'sign-ified' it by the angel unto his servant John." The "sign-ifying" was important to John in the life of our Lord, for what Jesus did was as much an opening, a revelation, of spiritual truth as what he said and what he taught.

For example, John 2 presents the miracle of the Lord turning the water into wine. At the wedding in Cana of Galilee there were six large earthenware containers. Each one of them held about three firkens of water—that is, about thirty-two gallons. John explained that they were there for the purification of the guests. When the guests arrived, they washed their feet and hands in the containers. When the Lord performed the miracle at the wedding, he asked the servants to fill all six of the containers. Then he told the servants to bear them to the governor of the feast. When the governor of the feast tasted the water that had turned into wine, he said, "I never tasted wine like this in my life." That is the kind of wine that we shall drink at the marriage supper of the Lamb.

When the Lord instituted the Lord's Supper he said; "I will not drink henceforth of this fruit of the vine, until that day when I drink it new with you in my Father's kingdom" (Matt. 26:29). When John observed that the Lord turned the water into wine, he says that Jesus began using *semeia*, "signs" in Cana of Galilee. What Jesus did was a spiritual revelation. Those six earthenware containers were first filled up. John saw in that sign that in Christ, the law was fulfilled. No jot, no tittle shall fail or fall; but all of the law shall be faithfully kept. The ordinances and judgments that were written against us are all abolished in Christ.

"And bear unto the governor of the feast" the new wine, for this is the new hope, the new promise, the new covenant in the blood and life of our Lord. The Lord did not place wine in an old wineskin that would break; nor did He place a patch on an old garment that would tear. His wine is new. It is glorious, heavenly, from God, a gospel, the good news. When John saw that, it was a sign to him.

Let us look at the feeding of the five thousand. The other three gospels reported the feeding of the five thousand, calling it a "miracle." But not John. He called the feeding of the five thousand a sign. In John 6 we read that Jesus spoke to the multitude the message of the bread of life. Our Lord said: "Verily, verily, I say unto you, Except ye eat the flesh of the Son of man, and drink his blood, ye have no life in you" (John 6:53). What Jesus presented was a sign, a great spiritual revelation.

Jesus Died of a Broken Heart

What sign did John see in blood and water when he said: "I saw out of His side blood and water flow forth. I bear record and I know that my record is true that ye might believe" (author's paraphrase)? It is this: The Lord died of a broken heart, a ruptured heart. In my reading of men who comment on this passage, there are some who will say it was a miracle and inexplicable that blood and water should have flowed out together from the side of our Lord.

In talking to a gifted physician one time, I asked him about the anatomical construction of the human heart and about the death of Jesus. The physician replied:

> Around the heart there is a pericardium, the cardiac sac. The heart beats in that sac. It lubricates the heart and keeps it from brushing and throbbing against the lungs. If the heart is ruptured, it will collapse and the blood will pour out into the pericardium. The sac can extend until it covers the entire thoracic cavity. Blood is about 55 percent serum and about 45 percent red coagulum. It can separate. What happened with our Lord was that on the cross His heart broke. When He died the heart collapsed, and the blood gushed out into the pericardium and separated. When the soldier came and thrust his spear through the side into the heart of our Lord, he pierced the pericardiac sac. When he drew out the spear, it was followed by a fountain of blood and water. The crimson and the life of our Lord poured out into the earth.

When John saw that he said, "It is a sign." In the first epistle he wrote of it: "This is he that came by water and blood" (1 John 5:6). The water is a sign of the cleansing, saving gospel grace of the Son of God. It is a sign of the Word that cleanses and saves us. He began his Gospel with the statement: "In the beginning was the Word, and the Word was with God, and the Word was God.

The same was in the beginning with God.

And the Word was made flesh, and dwelt among us (and we beheld his glory, the glory as of the only begotten of the Father), full of grace and truth" (John 1:1-2,14).

The water is a sign of the cleansing, saving Word, God manifest in the flesh. The Bible speaks of it in John 15:3: "Now ye are clean through the word which I have spoken unto you." In Ephesians 5:26 the apostle Paul said, "That he might sanctify and cleanse it with the washing of water by the word."

The Word of God, the spoken Word, the written Word, the incarnate Word, the Word of God spoken, preached, and delivered always has a salubrious, cleansing, and healthful effect upon the people. There is no man who can hear the gospel of Jesus Christ and not feel somehow that he needs to be washed, to be better, to be saved. That is the water that came forth from our Lord—the saving, cleansing of the blessed gospel message of Jesus!

The Atoning Blood

In 1 John 1:7 we read, "And the blood of Jesus Christ his Son cleanseth us from all sin." The blood of atonement, the blood of expiation, the blood of forgiveness, the blood that covers over and from God's sight and judgment all of the sin of our lives washes us clean and white.

So many of our hymns express how the blood of Jesus washes us pure without spot.

> What can wash away my sin?
> Nothing but the blood of Jesus;
> What can make me whole again?
> Nothing but the blood of Jesus.
> Oh, precious is the flow
> That makes me white as snow;
> No other fount I know,
> Nothing but the blood of Jesus.

In Ephesians 5 Paul avowed that out of the side of our Lord was born the church. He gave an illustration. Just as Eve was taken out of the side of Adam, out of the side of our Lord God took his bride, the church. That is, we are born in His sobs, in His cries, in His tears, in

His death, in His cross, and in His sufferings and blood. That is what John saw when he saw the blood and water flow out of our Lord when the Roman spear was withdrawn.

Lord, how is it that we could be so loved of God that Jesus should die for us? "This do in remembrance of me." Bread, His body so torn. Blood, the crimson of His life so poured out that we might live. O blessed gospel of the crimson flow!

12
The Blood of the Cross

(Heb. 9:22)

Almost all things are by the law purged with blood; and without shedding of blood is no remission (Heb. 9:22).

The secular and material world is bold and blatant in its rejection of the gospel of atoning blood. They refuse and repudiate the whole message of redemption, stating their opposition bluntly, rudely, and brutally. They say if we have tractors to move mountains, we do not need faith. If we have penicillin, we do not need prayer. If we have positive thinking, we do not need salvation. If we have the state, we do not need the church. If we have manuals on science, we do not need the Bible. If we have an Edison or an Einstein, we do not need Jesus. They define life altogether in secular and material nomenclature.

The Christian Religion Is a Message of Redemption

The gospel of the Son of God addresses itself to a far deeper need of humanity than penicillin, government, or manuals of science. The Christian faith addresses itself to the need for regeneration, the forgiveness of sins, a new life, a new heart, a new way, and a new day. The religion of Jesus Christ is one of deliverance and redemption from the judgment of sin. You see that in the very definition and description of the faith itself. The Christian faith is not, in the first place, an ethic, although it is ethical. It is not in the first place a theology, although it is theological. It is not in the first place reformational, although it has social, cultural, and political overtones. The religion of Jesus Christ is first, foremost, and always redemptive. He was delivered for our offenses, and he was raised for our justification (Rom. 4:25). You can see that in the aegis, the sign, and the symbol of the Christian religion.

The sign of the Christian faith is not a burning bush. It is not two tables of stone bearing the Ten Commandments. It is not a seven-branched lampstand. It is not a halo above a submissive head. It is not even a golden crown. The sign and the aegis of the Christian faith is always a cross—a cross in all of its naked hideousness, as the Romans would have it; the cross in all of its philosophical irrationality, as the Greeks would have it; but the cross in all of its saving power and efficacy, as Paul would have it. "God forbid that I should glory, save in the cross of our Lord Jesus Christ" (Gal. 6:14). This is the very epitome and summation of the redemptive message of Christ.

> Have you been to Jesus for the cleansing power?
> Are you washed in the blood of the Lamb?
> Are you fully trusting in His grace this hour?
> Are you washed in the blood of the Lamb?

The Descent and Sufferings of Our Lord

Our minds can hardly enter into the most significant and dramatic of all of the events in human history—the descent of our Lord from the highest glory to the lowest humiliation, the immeasurable distance between His throne in heaven and the ignominy of His cross in the earth. Down and down and down did the Lord descend until He was made in the likeness of a man, made out of the dust of the ground, a slave, poor even among the poor. He was finally executed in a manner reserved for the criminal, raised between heaven and earth, as though He were rejected by men and scorned by God, reviled and abused. As though abuse were not vile enough, they covered Him with spittle. As though spittle were not contemptuous enough, they crowned him with thorns. As though the thorns were not sharp enough, they drove great nails through His hands and His feet. As though the nails did not pierce deeply enough, they thrust Him through with a Roman spear, and the red, crimson of His life poured out. Even the sun in the sky refused to look upon such shame and suffering.

> Well might the sun in darkness hide,
> And shut his glories in,
> When Christ the mighty Maker died
> For man, the creature's sin.

What is the crucifixion of the Son of God on the cross? What happened on Golgotha, on Calvary? Is this a dramatic play like the *Agamemnon* of Aeschylus, or the tragedy of Shakespeare's *Macbeth* or *King Lear*? Is it a tragedy like Eugene O'Neill's *The Strange Interlude*? What is this that is happening on Calvary? Is it a historical tragedy like Socrates drinking the hemlock or Julius Caesar murdered at the foot of the statue of Pompey? Is it like the assassination of President Lincoln in Ford's Theater or like the tragedy that brought a cloud over Dallas in the assassination of President John Kennedy? What is this that happened on Calvary?

The Crucifixion Is the Judgment of God
Upon Our Sin

The death of Christ on the cross is the fruit and the result of our sins. Who killed the Lord Jesus? Who executed the Prince of Glory? Who nailed Him to the cross where He suffered until He died? Whose fault is that?

So many would answer, "God did it." Like Job's wife said to him when he fell into abject suffering, "Curse God and commit suicide." It is God's fault. He did it.

There are others who would say: "It is his own fault. He should have been a better manager. Had He been smart, He would not have been nailed to that tree. It is His own fault."

There are those who would say: "It is Judas' fault. He sold Him for thirty pieces of silver. He betrayed Him. It is Judas' fault. He did it."

There are those who say to this day: "It is the Jews' fault. They delivered Him. They accused Him. They encompassed His execution. It is their fault. They did it."

There are those who would say: "It is the Roman soldiers' fault. They are guilty of the death of the Lord. They did it. Who drove those nails through His hands? They did it. Who thrust the spear into His side? They did it. Who raised Him up between the earth and the sky? The Roman soldiers did it. They killed Him."

It is remarkable that each one disavows the guilt of the Lord's crucifixion. According to one tradition, when Pilate was recalled, he committed suicide, and they flung his body into Lake Lucerne. That is why just beyond the city of Lucerne there is a tall, towering mountain called Mt. Pilatus, Mt. Pilate. Legend says that in the mist of the twilight of every evening, the peasants see Pontius Pilate rise from the depths of the sea and wash his hands in the clear blue water of Lake Lucerne. "I am guiltless of the blood of this just man. I did not do it."

Then the Jews did it. They are Christ-killers. They crucified Him. Without exception, the Jew cries, "Would you bring the blood of this man upon us and upon our children? We did not do it."

Then surely it was the Roman soldiers. They executed him. But the Roman soldiers would stand in attention before you and say: "We are men under authority, and we but carried out the mandates and the commandments of the Roman government. We are soldiers obeying orders. We did not do it."

Then who did? Who is responsible for the crucifixion of the Son of God? Who ultimately must stand at the judgment bar accused?

It must be that we all had a part. My sins pressed upon his brow that crown of thorns. My sins drove through His hand those jagged nails. My sins thrust that spear into his heart. My sins nailed the Lord Jesus to the tree. That is the first meaning of the death of our Lord. It is the fruit and the judgment upon our sins.

The Death of Christ Is the Atonement of God for Our Sins

What is the meaning of the death of our Lord? This is God's redemption for our souls. This is God's way for our salvation. This is God's answer to our sins. This is the Lord's reply to Job when Job cried, "I have sinned, O God, what shall I do?" This is the answer to the cry of Macbeth, "Will all great Neptune's ocean wash this blood Clean from my hands?" This is the reply of the ancient old-time hymn that our forefathers used to sing:

> What can wash away my sin?
> Nothing but the blood of Jesus;
> What can make me whole again?
> Nothing but the blood of Jesus.
>
> Oh! precious is the flow
> That makes me white as snow;
> No other fount I know,
> Nothing but the blood of Jesus.

What is the meaning of that cross? This is the Lamb slain from before the foundation of the world. This is the blood of the Passover Lamb, for the Lord had said, "When I see the blood, I will pass over you." This is the Suffering Servant of Isaiah 53:6, "The Lord hath laid on him the iniquity of us all." This is the great redemption of the Lord God through all time and history. This is the pivotal moment in human story toward which all God's sovereign efforts finally found their ultimate consummation.

So Jesus bowed His head on the cross and cried, "It is finished!" The drops of blood that poured out from the cross to the dust of the ground whispered to the grass, saying, "It is finished!" The grass whispered to the herbs, "It is finished!" The herbs whispered to the trees, "It is finished!" The trees whispered to the birds in the branches, "It is finished!" The birds spiraling upwards to the clouds cried, "It is finished!" The clouds spoke to the stars in the sky, "It is finished!" The stars in the sky cried to the angels in heaven, "It is finished!" The angels in glory went up and down the streets of the heavenly city echoing this glad refrain, "It is finished!" The crucifixion of our Lord was God's redemption for the sin of the world.

The Cross Is the Message of Our Salvation

This is not only the death of our Lord, this is not only the result and the judgment upon our sin, it is not only God's redemptive plan for the ages, but the cross is the symbol of our hope in glory. In the words of John McCrae:

> In Flanders fields the poppies blow,
> Between the crosses, row on row.

Wherever men have fallen in the faith, there will you see a cross placed by the grave. It is a sign of our faith, of our promised heaven in the world to come. The arms of that cross are extended wide, wide as the world is wide. As far as the West goes West and the East goes East, just so far are the arms of the cross extended. In their embrace, all of us can find refuge, forgiveness, salvation, and hope. This hath God done for us.

Experiences in the beginning of my pastoral ministry made such indelible impressions on me. One of those experiences that I shall never forget was my first funeral.

In my little country church was a poor tenant farmer and his wife. They were young people who had been married just a little while. They had their first baby, a little boy. They sent for me because their baby was tragically ill. I went to a poor shack of a house, in the days of the depression. In the middle of the room lay a little baby in convulsions. As I watched sorrowfully, the baby died.

We held the memorial service. After the service, they took the little casket and put it on the bed of a truck. The couple could not afford any kind of service. In my little car, next to me sat the little mother, and on the other side the young father.

As we drove down the country road following the truck which bore the casket, the mother began to cry unconsolably. The young husband put his arm around her, and holding her as near and dear as he could, he said: "There, there, sweetheart. Do not cry. Jesus has our little boy, and He will take care of him for us. Some day He will give him back to us again." At the cemetery we buried the casket in a little grave with a barbed-wire fence around it. Do you know what we placed at the end of that little mound? We placed a cross and drove it into the ground.

The cross is a sign of our hope, our faith, our commitment to Jesus. Every word that He said He will faithfully keep. Every promise that He made will be faithfully kept for us. No word of our Lord will fall to the ground. He is able and mighty to save. That is our Lord, our Savior, our Redeemer, who died for our offenses and was raised for our justification. With what infinite gladness, gratitude, praise, and thanksgiving does the Christian lift up his head in the name of the Lord who died for us, who is able to save us, and who some day will present us before the throne of his glory without spot or blemish, washed clean and white in the blood of the Lamb!

13
Can Christ Make Good His Claims?

(Matt. 27:43)

> He trusted in God; let him deliver him now, if he will have him: for he said, I am the Son of God (Matt. 27:43).

Is Christ Jesus what He said He was and can He do what He said He could? The answer to that question is very easy for two reasons.—(1) We have the Holy Scriptures as a witness; and (2) we have two thousand years of Christian testimonies. In that length of time and in reading these holy pages, we have no timidity of hesitancy in making some great avowals concerning our Lord Christ today.

First, is He what He said He was? There never was a teacher, philosopher, poet or author, who ever spoke the words that He spoke. Is what He said true? On the day of the cross as they all walked up and down in front of Him, mocking Him, this is one of the things that they cried: "He trusted in God. Let God deliver Him now if He will have Him, for He said, 'I am the Son of God'." Is that true? He claimed God to be His Father, that He was born of the Holy Spirit, conceived in the womb of a virgin, that He was the Son of God. Is that true?

An infidel one time said, "What would you think if a young woman, pregnant, were to come to you and say, 'This child has no earthly father. It is conceived of the Holy Spirit. I am a virgin.' Would you believe her? What would you say?" The answer I would make is this: If that virgin came to me and if her child had been foretold in prophecy from before the foundation of the earth, if when the child was born the angels in heaven sang and praised the Lord, if when the child grew to manhood He spoke words and did miracles as no man had ever done, and if after He was crucified the third day He was raised from the dead, if He had ascended into heaven where He presides over an increasing and glorious kingdom of converts, if the girl had a child like that, I would without hesitation say God was His Father.

Napoleon Bonaparte was approached by a man who said, "I am a Messiah. I am founding a new religion, but I am having difficulty getting men to believe in me." Napoleon answered: "Why, that would be very simple. Just get yourself to be born of a virgin and be crucified and the third day rise from the dead and you will have no problem getting people to believe in you."

The marvelous and incomparable witness of heaven to this child and the work that He did and the words that He said which are unequaled in human literature and the marvel of His resurrected life felt and known among us today, bear witness to the truth of His claim: "I am the Son of God."

The Marvelous Words of Our Lord

Again our Lord said: "I am the light of the world; he that followeth me shall not walk in darkness, but shall have the light of life." Is He the Light of the world? I listened one time to a group of chaplains. I was speaking at a national convocation presided over by the chief of staff of our chaplains. There was a little group of them who had worked and ministered together in the South Pacific in World War II. They were recounting some of their experiences in the islands of the South Seas. As I listened to that chief of chaplains and some of the men who were with him in that arena of war, I was overwhelmed by what those men said. They spoke again and again of American soldiers who were converted by natives in those islands whose grandfathers had been cannibals. Oh, the marvelous light and glory that had come to those Samoans and Polynesians and South Sea Islanders by the preaching of the Gospel of the Son of God! "I am the light of the world," said the Christ.

One day I sat in Hiroshima by the side of a general in the Japanese army. He was then employed to be a Japanese teacher of young missionaries. By law, no man who had led in the Japanese war was allowed any place of prominence. Those men in the Nippon army and navy who fought in World War II were assigned to menial positions. This general of the army was teaching language to one of our Southern Baptist Missionary couples. To my great surprise, he was a Christian. As I sat by his side at a breakfast table, I asked him, "How is it that you, being a general, a member of the highest military command in the army, became a Christian?" He replied: "In our campaigns to overrun China, I looked at my men and armies, full of violence, blood and terror. Wherever we went in China, I also met the Christian missionaries and their work was one of love and ministry, building hospitals, gathering orphans, teaching the word of the love of God. I could not hide it from my face, or my mind and I became a Christian." "I am the light of the world," said our living Lord.

In making a mission tour around the earth, mostly in third world nations, I was overwhelmed by the depths of poverty, ignorance, disease and despair among the billions of the poor of the world. But wherever I went, there did I see the little church with its spire pointed toward heaven and by the side of the church, a school, and by the side of the school, an orphan's home, and by the side of the orphan's home, a Christian hospital. "I am the light of the world," said our Lord.

Is He what He said He was? The most profound sentence ever uttered by a man is this: "I am the resurrection, and the life: and he that believeth in me though He were dead, yet shall he live. Whosoever liveth and believeth in me shall never die." Is that true? The ancient world had a horror of death. To the ancient Greeks, it was a land of darkness beyond the cold and sullen River Styx. Even to the ancient Hebrew, it was an undefined region of darkness—the grave. But our Lord brought life and immortality to light. "I am the resurrection and the life," said our Lord. He took the sting out of death and He took victory from the grave.

In our Savior, death is now only for the physical frame, just a sleeping in Jesus. No fear, no dread, no foreboding, no terror, no horror, just going to sleep in the Lord. There is a Greek word, *koimao* which means "to fall asleep." The substantive of the word is *koimate-*

rion, "sleeping place." When you take the Greek word and spell it out in English, it comes out cemetery. That is a Christian word, invented by them to refer to the place where they laid their beloved dead away—asleep in Jesus.

The ancient Romans burned their dead. In urns they would stash them away in idol temples. But to the Christians it was unthinkable to have burned the body of our Lord. Tenderly and carefully the sorrowing disciples of Jesus wound in linen His body with one hundred pounds of spices and lovingly laid it away. So the Christians in Rome, in subterranean passages that they called catacombs, laid their loved ones away. The Christian is asleep in Jesus. His soul, spirit, and conscious life is with God. Wherever Jesus is, there we are when we die, awaiting the great resurrection day when God shall give us back this physical house, this tabernacle resurrected, glorified. Until then, we are at home with Him. "In my Father's house are many mansions . . . I go to prepare a place for you." To the Christian, death is a going to be with the Lord.

> I'll sing you a song of that beautiful land,
> The far away home of the soul,
> Where no storms ever beat on the glittering strand,
> While the years of eternity roll.

"I am the resurrection, and the life: he that believeth in me, though he were dead, yet shall he live: and whosoever liveth and believeth in me shall never die."

What Jesus Is Able to Do

We turn now to what He said He should do. Is He able to do what He said that He could? He said when He cleansed the temple, "Destroy this temple and in three days I will raise it up." To them it was an impossible word. They remembered it. At His trial they quoted it as blasphemous. When he died on the cross, they flung that claim into His teeth: "Thou that destroyest the temple, and buildest it in three days, save thyself." When He was dead and wrapped in a winding sheet and laid in the sepulchre of Joseph of Arimathaea, they went to Pilate and said: "'Sir, we remember that that deceiver said, while he was yet alive, After three days I will rise again. Command therefore that the sepulchre be made sure until the third day, lest his disciples come by night, and steal him away, and say unto the people, He is risen from the dead: so the last error shall be worse than the first.' Pilate said unto them, 'Ye have a watch: go your way, make it as sure as ye can.' So they went, and made the sepulchre sure, sealing the stone, and setting a watch.'" But the third day an angel came and broke that seal and rolled away that stone and in contempt, sat upon it. The Lord of Life walked forth, glorious, immortalized, transfigured.

Can He do what He said He could do? He said to a man who was an invalid, "Thy sins be forgiven thee." His critics said: "He blasphemes. Who can forgive sins but God?" That is correct. Only God can forgive sins. The Lord replied, "In order that you may know that the Son of Man hath power in this earth to forgive sins, Rise, take up thy bed and walk." The man arose, picked up his bed, and walked. To raise a man from the dead, as to forgive his sins, is in the power and prerogative of our living Lord.

Walking down a street in Chicago, I heard singing. I stopped and walked in. It was the Pacific Garden Mission. I sat down. I never saw such a motley group in my life, nor did I ever witness a service like that. Out of the gutter, out of the literal depths of depravity and hell were they there, a host of them. They were singing songs about Jesus. They were writing poems about Jesus. They were testifying about the Lord Jesus. They were new men and women in Him.

Can He do what He says He is able to do? He said, "I am come that they might have life, and that they might have it more abundantly." Can He give us abundant, overflowing life? Does He, can He? Oh, the fullness of the gladness of the new life that we have in Christ Jesus! If success is my life, to fail is to be miserable. If popularity is my life, to be poor is to be miserable. If popularity is my life, to be passed by is miserable. If to be young is my life, to be old is to be miserable. If health is my life, to be sick is to be miserable; if liberty is my life, to be in prison is to be miserable. But if Christ is my life, whether sick, old, imprisioned or forgotten, I am happy in Him.

I entered once a home of care,
And penury and want were there,
But joy and peace withal.
I asked the aged mother whence
Her helpless widowhood's defense,
She answered, "Christ Jesus is all."

I saw the martyr at the stake,
The flames could not his courage shake,
Nor death his soul appall.
I asked him whence his strength was given,
He looked triumphantly to heaven and answered,
"Christ is all."

I stood beside the dying bed,
Where lay a child with aching head,
Waiting Jesus' call.
I saw him smile, 'twas sweet as May,
And as his spirit passed away,
He whispered, "Christ is all."

I dreamed that hoary time had fled,
The earth and sea gave up their dead,
A fire dissolved this ball.
I saw the church's ransomed throng,
I caught the burden of their son,
'Twas this: that Christ is all.

"For to me to live is Christ, and to die is gain."

14
How the Death of Christ Saves Us

(John 3:14-15)

> And as Moses lifted up the serpent in the wilderness, even so must the Son of man be lifted up:
>
> That whosoever believeth in him should not perish, but have eternal life (John 3:14-15).

There are many theories of the atonement (how the death of Christ saves us). Throughout the centuries men have tried to expound the reason for the efficacious offering of the Son of God. There is the patristic explanation, that of the early church fathers and their penal theory. There is the Anselmic theory that the atonement honored God's sense of justice and righteousness. Another theory was the Socinian theory, that the death of Christ was that of an example, a paragon that he died as a martyr dies or a hero dies. There were also the Grotian and the Bushnellian theories.

While I was in the seminary, one of my minors was the atonement. Even after studying the atonement for two years and after I had passed a doctor's examination on the subject, I felt that the mystery of the death of Christ was as unfathomable and as inexplicable as the day that I began the survey.

There is a mystery in the death of Christ that the mind cannot enter. There is something in God, in the Holy Spirit, and in Christ in the forgiveness of our sins that is a mystery into which only a mind that could equal the mind of God could ever be commensurate. But there are some things that a rational human being, one who can understand and sense, can see. We can see what God is like, what God does, and how God does it—which is all that a human being can see anyway, for no man can explain anything. He merely sees and describes what he sees, but the intricate details that lie back of its being, we do not enter into; we just see the result.

So the marvelous mystery—inexplicable, unfathomable, indescribable—of the atoning grace of God and the death of Christ is beyond what we are able to encompass in theology or in sermon.

There Is Death in Sin

Here is one thing we can see. There is something in God that put these two together—sin and death. God welded the link together in the beginning, and no man has ever been able to unweld the iron chain that steadfastly and eternally holds them. Sin and death: "The wages of sin is death" (Rom. 6:23); "The soul that sinneth it shall die" (Ezek. 18:20); "In the day that thou eatest thereof thou shalt surely die" (Gen. 2:17). When God pronounces judgment upon transgression the result is death. The day one sins, he begins to die.

But the same Lord God who pronounced that judgment upon our sins—physical death, moral death, spiritual death, the second death, eternal death—also did something else. God said that atonement could be vicariously made. Somebody else could die in our stead. Somebody else could suffer in our death. If that vicarious suffering were of a nature as to satisfy God, we who have sinned can go free.

Sometimes the Bible describes that redemption in terms of a ransom. A slave is taken into captivity and is sold. We in sin are like that. As the Scriptures say of us, "[We are] sold under sin" (Rom. 7:14). We are in the bondage of sin. But somebody could pay our debt; somebody could ransom us; somebody could buy us back. That is a presentation in the Scriptures of the grace of Christ. The Scriptures say, "Ye are not your own . . . Ye are bought with a price" (1 Cor. 6:19-20). "For the Son of Man came not to be ministered unto, but to minister, and to give his life a ransom for many" (Mark 10:45). Somebody else can pay our debt and our penalty, and we can go free.

Most of the time our redemptive salvation is presented in the Bible under the figure, the picture, the typology, and the symbolism of one who is shedding blood—that is, pouring out his life for us.

In the days of the Passover God said, "My angel of death will visit the land of Egypt, but it shall be that if there is blood sprinkled on the lintels and on the doorposts, the angel of death will pass over; and there will be life in that home" (author's paraphrase). All that a man had to do to be saved, to be delivered from the judgment that night in Egypt, was to find safety under the blood. God did the necessary action. When the angel saw the blood, he passed over. Vicariously an offering is presented—in this instance, a lamb.

The Day of Atonement presented this same picture of atoning grace. Two sacrificial animals were chosen; one was slain, its blood caught in a basin. The high priest entered into the holy of holies beyond the veil and took the blood and sprinkled it upon the propitiatory, the mercy seat. Then the second sacrificial animal was brought before the high priest, who had come out of the holy place. The high priest laid both of his hands on top of the animal and confessed all the sins of the people. Then the animal (called the *scapegoat*, for in its atoning blood human sins were taken away) was taken out to a place far away and driven off. That, like the picture, was in the whole sacrificial system. Twice every day the lamb was slain and offered as a burnt sacrifice for the sins of the people. Mostly it will be under the figure, which God will teach us, that in the shedding of blood there is remission of sin.

The Lamb of God, Jesus, Pays Our Debt of Sin

If our blood were shed, we could not atone for anyone else because we ourselves are sinners. When we die, we just pay the penalty for our own sins. But all of the sacrificial system of the Old Testament—the Day of Atonement, the Passover feast, and so forth—all of those were pictures and types of him who was the Lamb of God and the Lord in heaven. Our Father so values the priceless life of Jesus that the sacrifice of the Prince of Glory is commensurate with all of the sins of all the world. As in the days of the Passover, if one was under the blood, God gave him life for death.

And so it is with us. God so values and prizes the blood of Jesus that if one trusts in his son, God considers the atoning death of our

Lord as more than grace sufficient to wash away all of our sins, "For the wages of sin is death; but the gift of God is eternal life through Jesus Christ" (Rom. 6:23).

In Romans 5:1-10 we read:

> Therefore being justified by faith, we have peace with God through our Lord Jesus Christ: By whom also we have access by faith into this grace wherein we stand, and rejoice in hope of the glory of God. And not only so, but we glory in tribulations also: knowing that tribulation worketh patience; And patience, experience; and experience, hope: And hope maketh not ashamed; because the love of God is shed abroad in our hearts by the Holy Ghost which is given unto us. For when we were yet without strength, in due time Christ died for the ungodly. For scarcely for a righteous man will one die: yet peradventure for a good man some would even dare to die. But God commendeth his love toward us, in that, while we were yet sinners, Christ died for us. Much more then, being now justified by his blood, we shall be saved from wrath through him. For if, when we were enemies, we were reconciled to God by the death of his Son, much more, being reconciled, we shall be saved by his life."

God so values the death of his Son that if anyone will trust in Jesus, God says that trust is equal, all-sufficient for the washing away of all of his sins.

The Holy Spirit has the power to apply that message to the human heart. Let me illustrate that miracle of the Holy Spirit by a comparison. One could study extensively about the martyrs, the heroes, the Nathan Hales who say, "I only regret that I have but one life to lose for my country." We admire and praise God for a patriot like Nathan Hale. The sacrifice of men like him made our nation what it is. The pouring out of blood for freedom, for liberty, and for the protection of our homes and families has been the story of martyrdom, bloodshed, and heroic dedication through the years.

When I speak of the martyr's death and the hero's death, the people who listen say: "What a noble dedication. We ought to appreciate the liberties and freedoms which have come to us through their sacrifices." But in the gratitude and admiration of that sacrifice and dedication, no one is ever convicted of his sins. No one would be drawn to a new life in repentance, in confession, and in faith. But when a man anywhere presents the death, the sobs, the tears, the flowing wounds of Jesus, God's Holy Spirit does something in the hearts of the people. There is a conviction of sin. We cry, "I am not what I ought to be; I am not what I could be; by God's grace I am not what I am going to be." There is a conviction of sin in our hearts. We sense our shortcomings, our derelictions, our failures, and our transgressions. That is the work of the Holy Spirit.

The Holy Spirit does something else. He points to the cross; he points to Jesus; he points to the Lamb of God. And he does it in wooing grace, in loving invitation and appeal. "Look," the Holy Spirit says. That is why any time there is a teaching that emphasizes the Holy Spirit alone, it is a teaching the opposite of what the New Testament doctrine is—for the Lord said, "The Holy Spirit shall not speak of himself; he will not draw attention to himself." The work of the Holy Spirit serves someone else.

The Holy Spirit exalts Jesus, points to Jesus, and brings our hearts to Jesus. When a man speaks about the grace and the love of God in Christ Jesus, something happens to him. We look and look and look; then one day we see. We listen and listen; then one day we hear. The gospel message is pressed to the heart of the person hungry for fulfillment by the power of the Holy Spirit.

Sometimes I see people weep. Why do they cry? Just thinking about the Lord, just looking again, just seeing Jesus. Almost always there will be an experience in the life of a child when the child will cry before the Lord. Why? Just looking at Jesus, the power of the cross of Christ. That is the work of the Holy Spirit. God is so near and so dear that we are overcome. Not only does God count the blood of Christ all-sufficient for our sins; and not only does the Holy Spirit press the message of saving grace to our hearts; but we sense and feel his presence. I have always thought that far more important than an intellectual understanding of the death of Christ is the feeling of his presence in our souls, the realization of him in our deepest hearts. This he did for me.

Saved by the Intercessory Life of Our Lord

God also says, "For if when we were enemies [sinners, recalcitrants, unrepentants, unregenerates], we were reconciled to God by the death of his Son (God says that in Christ our sins are all washed away and that the debt has been paid), much more, being reconciled, we shall be saved by his life" (Rom. 5:9). By "his life" Paul was referring to the Lord's resurrected life. If in the cross of Christ—if in the death of Jesus our sins are all paid, we have been reconciled to God, God is favorable toward us, and he has forgiven us and welcomes us—then we are even more certainly assured of our salvation. I think of that in three ways.

First, he comes to live in our hearts and in our homes. Jesus is here. We can feel and sense his presence. The Lord said: "Behold, I stand at the door and knock: if any man hear my voice, and open the door, I will come in to him and will sup with him, and he with me" (Rev. 3:20). We can have fellowship with God. If we have been reconciled by the death of his Son, much more shall we be saved by his life.

Second, not only is Christ with us living in our hearts; but the Scriptures say, "He is able also to save them to the uttermost that come unto God by him seeing he ever liveth to make intercession for them" (Heb. 7:25). He prays for us and intercedes for us. He pulls for us; he helps us. He is in heaven, and our Lord bows down his ear to hear his people when they pray. He reaches down with helping hands of encouragement, sympathy, and understanding.

> What a friend we have in Jesus,
> All our sins and griefs to bear!
> What a privilege to carry
> Everything to God in prayer!

Third, in the final hours of my death, who can go with me across that dark and swollen river? Can you? When that hour comes, I will have to face it alone. That is why it is such a tragedy to die lost. Nobody to help, no Savior, no Lord. Just dying alone.

In the closing of *The Pilgrim's Progress*, when the time came for

Pilgrim to cross the swollen river, the trumpet sounded on the other side and one of God's saints went home. When we die we have a coronation day. It is the greatest day and the sublimest hour of our life, for Christ is with us to receive us to himself. Our home is there; our inheritance is there; and our Lord is there. We are saved by his life, received into glory, welcomed by his precious hands. As one of our eloquent preachers used to say, "The pierced hands of Jesus who opened for us the doors of grace shall open for us the gates of glory." Oh, what it means to be a Christian, to love the Lord!

15
The Witness Against Him

(Matt. 26:59)

> Now the chief priests, and elders, and all the council, sought false
> witness against Jesus, to put him to death (Matt. 26:59).

No more panoramic view of human nature is it possible for us to see than to look upon all of the participants of the day of the cross. This hour we shall consider those who witnessed against Him, His enemies. Goodness, culture, altruism and philanthropy are skin deep; underneath is the raw, crude, carnal, unregenerate human nature. They say, "Beauty is skin deep, but ugly is to the bone." This is true about the goodness of the human race; it is a veneer, a polished exterior. Always underneath lurks the possibility of every terror and violence known to the human heart.

Look at Lebanon, the jewel of the Levant. Beirut, a beautiful city with prosperous and affluent merchants, is today warring in hatred and bitterness. Bombing, strafing and murdering are decimating every faction. That is human nature. But we see it most poignantly on the day of the cross.

"All the chief priests and elders of the people took counsel against Jesus." It seemed that the whole human race looked in despicable bitterness on Jesus of Nazareth. In Him was fulfilled that sad prophecy of Isaiah 53:3, "He is despised and rejected of men; a man of sorrows, and acquainted with grief: and we hid as it were our faces from him; he was despised, and we esteemed him not." His own family was that way. John is careful to record that His brothers did not believe in Him. That was why on the cross Jesus committed His mother to John; her own sons and the brothers of Jesus did not believe on Him. John records that upon one occasion the family came to take Him home by force, for they said, "He is beside Himself." That is a nice way of saying: "He is mad. He has lost His mind." His own family looked with despair upon Him.

When He came to His own townspeople, the place called Nazareth in which He grew up, they listened to the marvelous words that fell from His lips and said in anger; "Whence hath this man wisdom? Is this not the carpenter?" Others said, "Is this not the carpenter's son? Are not His sisters and brothers and Mary His mother with us?" They were offended by Him and took Him to the brow of the hill on which their city was built to cast Him down headlong to death.

His nation, as such, rejected Him. "He came unto His own, and His own received Him not." The scribes, elders, Pharisees and the whole leadership of the people were united in denouncing and destroying the Son of God. They finally put a price on His head and eventually encompassed His execution. Why did they so find fault in Him? What were their criticisms of Him? We can name four.

Why Jesus Was Hated and Rejected

(1) They said He was a friend of publicans and sinners. Matthew, whom the Lord chose to be one of His apostles, was one of those hated tax collectors. The Lord showed Himself a friend to those who were outcasts from the covenant of Israel's kindness, acceptability, and hospitality. Jesus also ate with them. He identified Himself with them. Righteousness usually repels people who are sinful, but these derelicts gathered around the Lord Jesus like flies would gather around sticky paper. He attracted sinners. They loved to listen to Him. They found a marvelous hope in Him. The self-righteous Pharisees, seeing that, hated Him. He was a friend of publicans and sinners.

(2) He healed on the Sabbath Day. To the Lord Jesus, any day was a good day to do good. Monday or Thursday, Saturday or Sunday, any day was a good day to help people who needed encouragement and remembrance. If the ox fell in the ditch, no one hesitated to take it to drink. But to heal on the Sabbath Day was not to be done. They hated Him for it.

(3) They said the Son of God was a glutton and a wine bibber; that is, He was gregarious and convivial. He liked to be with people. If you had a dinner at the church, you would see Him there. I have looked through the life of Christ and found an unusual thing; He never turned down an invitation. They made an ugly distinction between Jesus who was with the people and John the Baptist who was out in the desert. They called John the prophet, but this Jesus they said was possessed with the devil. The Lord loved to be with saints and sinners alike and to be in their homes. He is that way still. In heaven there is a picture of the Lord: "Behold, I stand at the door, and knock: if any man hear my voice, and open the door, I will . . . come in to him, and will sup with him, and he with ME."

(4) He did not walk in the tradition of the elders. The tradition of the elders is the Halakhah and the Haggadhah, found in the Mishna and the two Gemaras. When it finally was written down, it comprises thousands and thousands and thousands of pages. In modern language we call it the Talmud. Jesus brushed it all aside. He lived and preached according to the word of God. Because He did not follow the tradition of the elders, they hated and despised Him and finally encompassed His death.

What the Enemies of Jesus Said About Him

With those who were witnesses against the Lord, that is HIS enemies, let us see what they said. First, let us look at Judas Iscariot. He is the one who betrayed Him. He was paid thirty pieces of silver, the price of a slave. Accepting the silver, he betrayed the Lord Jesus with a kiss. After the Lord was arrested, Judas came to those who had given him the thirty pieces of silver saying, "I have sinned, in that I have betrayed the innocent blood." He cast the thirty pieces of silver on the floor of the temple and went out and took his own life. When we read the confession of Judas, we think of all of those innocent victims which are types of the atoning death of our Lord from the days when the blood of Abel mingled with his sacrifice through the Passover Lamb, through all of the rituals in both tabernacle and temple. Every sacrificial victim, innocent and guiltless that was slain was a type of the innocent blood of our Lord Jesus Christ. Judas, who betrayed Him came saying: "I have sinned. I have betrayed the innocent blood."

The second witness is Pontius Pilate, the Roman procurator who delivered Him to execution. He said, "I find no fault in Him." Why did Pilate deliver Him to execution? The reason is very obvious. There were Senatorial provinces; that is, those that were under the direction of the Roman senate. Then there were Imperial provinces; that is, those that were under the aegis of the Roman Emperor. The difference in the two was this: if a province was peaceful, it was placed under the direction of the Roman senate. But if a province was volitive and likely to rebel, it was placed under the direction of the Roman Caesar, because Caesar controlled the army. The Caesar having the army, controlled the province. Judea was an Imperial province because it was volitive and full of restiveness, consequently it was controlled by the Caesar and the Roman legions. That meant that the procurator or governor was appointed not by the Senate but by the Roman Emperor. Pontius Pilate was an appointee of the Roman Caesar. Already drifting back to Rome were many things about Pontius Pilate that made the Roman Emperor unhappy and when those elders, thirsting after the blood of Christ, said "You are not a friend to Caesar if you let this man go," Pilate trembled and even though his wife sent him word, "Have thou nothing to do with this just man," he pronounced the sentence of death. He did this even though he found in Him no fault at all. Over Christ's head He wrote this inscription: "King of the Jews." The elders came to the governor and said: "Do not say He is the King of the Jews. Say that He said He was the King of the Jews." Pilate replied that famous word, "What I have written, I have written." He wrote the superscription in Hebrew, the language of the faith. He wrote it in Greek, the language of art, science, and literature. He wrote it in Latin, the language of law and government.

We turn now to the witness of those who delivered Him to death: the witness of the chief priests and scribes and elders. They said, "He saved others, Himself He cannot save." As they walked up and down mocking Him they said: "If thou be the king of the Jews, come down from the cross and we will believe. He saved others; Himself

He cannot save." When I read that and see it, I wish Jesus would have torn Himself from the wood and come down and struck terrified horror in their hearts. But no, He could not do it if I am to be saved. When He is taken down from the cross, it will not be some superman; it will be a limp and lifeless corpse whom they wrapped in a winding sheet and laid in a tomb. You see, if I am to live, He has to die. If my sins are to be washed away, it must be in a fountain of blood, the crimson of His life that was poured out on the earth.

The Moving Death of Christ on the Cross

Another witness: There were crucified with the Lord two malefactors. They were vile and vicious men whom the Roman government had condemned to death.

> And one of the malefactors which was hanged railed on him, saying, "If thou be Christ, save thyself and us." But the other answering rebuked him, saying, "Dost not thou fear God, seeing thou are in the same condemnation? And we indeed justly; for we receive the due reward of our deeds: but this man hath done nothing amiss." And he said unto Jesus, "Lord, remember me when thou comest into thy kingdom."

How did he know Jesus? This malefactor, taken out of prison and nailed to a tree by the side of the Lord, knew that the Son of God had done nothing amiss. How did he know about the coming kingdom? He knew it all by faith, by the eyes of the soul. I think the truest knowledge in the world is intuitive. It is something that God teaches us. It is knowledge such as we witness on the Mount of Transfiguration. Peter, James and John had never seen Moses. Moses had been dead for fourteen hundred years. They had never seen Elijah. Elijah had been dead for nine hundred years. But there the apostles knew and recognized them. How: By intuitive knowledge. It is the knowledge that God gives us. This intuitive knowledge God gives to a man when he comes face to face with Jesus Christ.

The last witness: "Now when the centurion, and they that were with him, watching Jesus, saw the earthquake, and those things that were done, they feared greatly, saying, Truly this was the Son of

God." He was a hardened Roman centurion. All of his life he had carried out these assignments of execution. But he never executed a man like that. His heart was filled with awe and wonder as he stood at the cross and saw Jesus die. I have a deep persuasion that any man who will be honest and right and fair and listen to God's spirit in his heart will come to the same conclusion as did this centurion— if he will just look, get a good look at the Son of God dying for us.

Do you remember the story of Bob Ingersol? He was a famous and learned unbeliever of the last century. He was riding on a train by the side of General Lew Wallace, who was the governor of New Mexico and who was also not a Christian. Ingersol said to Wallace, "Why do you not write a book that sets forth the truth about this deceiver, Jesus Christ?" Wallace said: "I had not thought for such a thing, but I believe I will." So he studied the life of our Lord, and became a great and devout Christian, and wrote one of the noblest books of faith of all time. It is called *Ben Hur*. Do you remember the subtitle? It is: *Ben Hur (A Story of the Christ)*.

That Roman centurion was just like that: looking at Jesus die, he found in Him the Son of God, our Saviour.

> My Jesus, I love Thee,
> I know Thou art mine,
> For Thee all the follies
> Of sin I resign;
> My gracious Redeemer,
> My Saviour art Thou;
> If ever I loved Thee,
> My Jesus, 'tis now.

16
The Glory of the Cross

(Gal. 6:14)

> But God forbid that I should glory, save in the cross of our Lord Jesus Christ, by whom the world is crucified unto me, and I unto the world (Gal. 6:14).

Let us now begin with Galatians 6:11: "Ye see how large a letter I have written unto you with mine own hand. As many as desire to make a fair shew in the flesh, they constrain you to be circumcised; only lest they should suffer persecution for the cross of Christ. For neither they themselves who are circumcised keep the law; but desire to have you circumcised, that they may glory in your flesh. But God forbid that I should glory, save in the cross of our Lord Jesus Christ, by whom the world is crucified unto me, and I unto the world" (Gal. 6:11-14).

In the text Paul makes a contrast between the Galatians who glory in the flesh (the Greek word is *kauchaomai*, "glory," "boast,") and his own humble, committed spirit that forbids that he should glory, save in the cross of Jesus Christ. The Galatians in their propensity and affinity for glorying in the flesh, for turning aside from the salvation provided by the love and mercy of God in Jesus, and for turning to sophisticated human teachers, thought that in self-righteousness and self-commendation they should save themselves before God.

In the third chapter of this book Paul addressed them, "O foolish Galatians, who hath bewitched you?" (v. 1a). I think that if we were to take the letter and the appeal of the apostle written in the first century and apply it today he would have said, "O foolish modernists, who has bewitched you that you should glory in the flesh, in human effort, in human speculation? But God forbid that I should glory save in the cross of our Lord Jesus Christ." The cross with all of its naked hideousness, as the Roman would have it; the cross with all of its philosophical irrationality, as the Greek would have it; the cross with all of its shame and suffering, as the scribe would have it; but the cross with all of its love and mercy and forgiveness, as Paul preached it.

> In the cross of Christ I glory,
> Towering o'er the wrecks of time;
> All the light of sacred story
> Gathers round its head sublime.

"God forbid that I should glory, save in the cross of our Lord Jesus Christ."

The Sign of the Cross as an Emblem of the Christian Faith

The cross is a sign, an aegis, an emblem of the Christian faith. The whole course of history turned in A.D. 300 when Constantine was converted. In the midst of a battle for the throne of the Caesars Constantine said, "At midday I saw a sign in the sky, a cross, and underneath these words: *'In hoc signo vinces,'* 'in this sign conquer'." Upon this occasion, as upon countless other occasions before, the sign of the Gospel of the Son of God is found in a cross.

The insignia of the Christian faith is not two tables of stone containing the commandments of God. It is not a sword, a scimitar, a star, or a galaxy. The insignia of the Christian faith is not a seven-branched lampstand or even a halo above a submissive head. Rather, the insignia of the Christian faith is a stark, rude, crude, rugged cross.

Sometimes visiting the Roman Colosseum I stand and look at what is the best example of the cross that I know. Unlike what we think of as a decoration on the top of a church or as an ornament to wear around our necks made of gold and silver and studded with precious stones, the cross in the Colosseum is as rugged a crossbeam as could be ingeniously devised. I am told that it was placed there many years ago in honor and in memory of the early Christians who lost their lives in that terrible arena.

The cross speaks a universal language. All men everywhere understand it. Some time ago I sat in a great throng against the background of a mountain of Bavaria, listening to the Passion Play in Oberammergau. The thousands of people in attendance were from every nationality, tongue, tribe, family, and language under the sun. The play was in German and there were many of us who could not follow it in the Germanic tongue. But I had the unusual and deep persuasion that as we sat there and watched the drama of the suffering and crucifixion of our Lord, every man in his own language and in his own tongue understood it. The cross speaks to human hearts everywhere in every nation, in every language, in every family, clan, and tribe under God's heaven.

The cross of Christ is not a mythical, romantic idea, symbol, or story. It is historical and factual. If we think of the reference to Christ in Josephus as an interpolation, there are just two early first-century references to the Lord Jesus. They are found in Suetonius and Tacitus, Latin historians, and in both instances they refer to the crucifixion of our Lord. The historical reference was occasioned by the burning of Rome. When the people began to point their fingers at Nero as having done it, in order to obviate the suspicion, he said the Christians did it. Now that necessitated the early Roman historian to describe who the Christians were, for it was a strange, unusual, and unknown sect. So both Suetonius and Tacitus say that the Christians were followers of a felon who was crucified in Judaea under Pontius Pilate.

The cross is the cruelest instrument of execution that the human mind has ever devised. No Roman citizen could be crucified. Death by crucifixion was reserved for felons, insurrectionists, criminals, and murderers. It was especially opprobrious to the Jews. The Apostle Paul in Galatians 3 quoting Deuteronomy 21, quotes Moses as saying, "Cursed is everyone who is hanged on a tree." In the story of the crucifixion of Christ we are told that when the even was come, the day the Lord was crucified, the Jews went to the procurator and asked that the crosses be taken down, for the pilgrims were coming into the city for the sacred Passover and the ghastly sight would be offensive to them.

But as horrible as it was to the Romans and as unthinkable as it was to the minds of the Jews, think of the shame that it bore to the pure, holy, undefiled, sinless Son of God. In crucifixion our blessed Lord was humiliated in two ways. One, they crucified Him naked. He was exposed before the whole world. The artists have been kind in drawing pictures of the Lord. Always they clothe Him, but actually He died naked. They gambled for His garments at the foot of the cross. Second, He was crucified between malefactors, between insurrectionists and murderers. In His life He was known as a friend of publicans and sinners, and in His death He was crucified with one on either side. In our Savior history and prophecy met, for the fifty-third chapter of Isaiah said that He would be numbered with transgressors. He became sin itself.

This was no ordinary crucifixion. There were thousands of Jews who had been crucified under the Roman emperors. The historians suggest that in the forty years between Pontius Pilate and Titus there were more than thirty thousand Jews who were crucified. When the Lord was eighteen years of age, in a village near Nazareth the Romans came to burn the town and to crucify everyone in it because the citizens had been accused of harboring zealots and insurrectionists. Jesus being nearby must have seen those crosses raised against the sky. It was a common sight in Palestine to see a Roman crucifixion. But the crucifixion of Jesus was not the same. The Roman centurion under whose surveillance the execution was carried out cried, saying, "This man surely was the Son of God."

> Well might the sun in darkness hide
> And shut his glories in,
> When Christ, the mighty Maker, died
> For man, the creature's sin.

The cross is a sign of the Gospel of the Christian faith.

The Cross Speaks of Man's Universal Depravity

Second, the cross is a sign and an emblem of the universal depravity of the human heart. If one would see what humanity is really like, look at the cross, cruel and merciless, dark and sinful. The Lord was born in Bethlehem. The gift of God in love to the world came in that little town of David. When the gift was made the angels sang and the stars were lowered like golden lamps from the sky. The shepherds worshiped and the wise men brought their gifts. Just five miles away is Jerusalem. Thirty-three years later the human family, humankind, gave back the gift of God's love in Christ Jesus on the point of a Roman spear. Who did that, who crucified the Lord? Who is responsible for His shameful, indescribably ignominious death? Who did that?

Well, there are many answers. Some say it is God's fault, that God did it. The wife of Job said to her husband, "Curse God and commit suicide." There are others who say it is His own fault. He should have been a better manager and a better planner, and He should have been shrewder. There are those who say that the Jews did it. There are those who say that the rulers did it. Some say Judas Iscariot did it. He sold Him. There are those who say Pontius Pilate did it—the weak, vacillating procurator who looked upon the miscarriage of Roman justice. There are those who say the soldiers did it. They platted the crown of thorns and they nailed Him to the tree. Who did it? Pontius Pilate washes his hands and says: "I did not do it. I am innocent of the blood of that just man." The Roman soldiers say, "We did not do it!" Who did it? Who slew the Son of glory? Who nailed Him to the cross? It must have been that we all had a part. We all did it. Our sins nailed Him to the tree and our sins pressed upon His brow the crown of thorns. We all did it.

A man one time said: "In a dream I saw the Savior. His back was bare and there was a soldier lifting up his hand and bringing down on His back that awful scorpion of nine tails, that awful cat-o-nine tails with its leather thongs and its pieces of iron woven into the leather. In the dream I rose and grasped his arm to hold it back. When I did, the soldier turned around in astonishment to look at me, and when I looked at him I recognized myself!" Who slew the Son of glory? We all did it. Our sins crucified the Prince of heaven. The cross is a universal sign of human depravity and human sin.

The Cross as a Sign of Our Hope of Heaven

The cross is, third, a sign and an emblem of our atonement and our salvation, our hope of glory. Christ died. How did He die? Why did He die? Did He die like Socrates, drinking the hemlock, a martyr to philosophical truth? Did He die like Julius Caesar, a hero in the senate before the cruel daggers of Brutus and Cassius? Did He die like the Agamemnon in Aeschylus carrying out the heroic assignment of the Greek nation against the Trojans? Did He die like Shakespeare's tragedy of King Lear? Did He die like Abraham Lincoln under the assassin's bullet in Ford's Theater in Washington? How did He die?

There is a divine meaning in the death of Christ. This is God's plan for our salvation. There is no pardon and peace apart from atonement. There is no remission of sins apart from the shedding of blood and there is no reconciliation without the payment of death. This is our atonement, our propitiation, our sacrifice for sin. This is our means of reconciliation to God. The cross to the Apostle Paul and to us is the same thing as the brazen serpent raised in the wilderness was to Moses and the children of Israel. It is a sign of universal love, mercy, forgiveness, and healing from the hands of God.

> Look and live, my brother, live!
> Look to Jesus now and live;
> 'Tis recorded in His Word, hallelujah!
> It is only that you "look and live."

The cross is a sign of our atonement. It is a sign of our forgiveness. It is a sign of God's inviting love, His invitation to pardon and forgiveness. It is an invitation to life. The cross has an upraised beam. Raised toward the sky, it points toward God in heaven. It has a lower part that touches the earth. God, reaching out His loving hand, extends it down even to us. It has crossarms and they go in either direction as far as the East goes East and as far as the West goes West. The arms of the cross are extended to the limits of the earth. It is the open invitation to all men everywhere to find life, liberty, forgiveness, mercy, and salvation in the atoning love, sobs, tears, suffering death of the Son of God. We are all welcome.

The arms of the cross extend to all mankind—to the Greek and to the Barbarian, to the Roman and to the provincial, to the Jew and to the Greek, to the bond and to the free, to the lettered and to the unlearned, to the rich and to the poor, to the wise and to the unwise, to the old and to the young, to the near and to those who are far off, to the good and to the not so good, to all of us does God extend wide His invitation. The world could never be the same again because our Lord died in it. It was this planet upon which Jesus spilled His sacred blood.

That cross is a sign of our hope of glory. If there is any tomorrow, if there is any heaven, if there is any God and life yet to be, the cross is a sign of that hope.

> If in Flanders Fields the poppies grow
> It will be between the crosses row to row.

Recently I passed by a large cemetery near Athens, Greece. It was filled with thousands of white crosses. As I looked at them I thought of many other cemeteries, especially American military cemeteries around the world, such as at Arlington, Virginia, in the Philippines, in the Hawaiian Islands, in France. Everywhere above that American boy who has fallen in battle our people erected a cross. Why? Because it is a hope. It is a prayer, it is a vision, it is a dream, it is an expectation, it is a promise, it is an assurance that God has prepared some better thing for us than what we know in the sorrow and tears of this life. If we have any hope, any forgiveness, any tomorrow, it lies in the atoning death of the Son of God.

I was in London one day standing in Charing Cross. Years ago the beloved wife of the King died far away from London. As the King tenderly and lovingly brought her body back to the great city, wherever her body rested in the long journey the King built a little chapel and he called it always by some kind of a cross, as the King's Cross, as Charing Cross. I was standing in Charing Cross in London and a fellow minister by my side said: "Let me tell you a story that happened here. There was a little girl in the city who lost her way. She just wandered around in the streets of London, crying heart-brokenly, pitiously. An English bobby saw the child wandering and stopped her to ask her why her sobbing. The child answered that she was lost and did not know how to find her way home. The bobby said to her, 'Do not cry. Sit down here by my side and we will find where you live, where home is.' So the bobby sat on the curb of the street and the little brokenhearted girl sat by his side. He said, 'Now I am going to ask you some places in London and you tell me if you recognize any of them. Piccadilly Circus?' 'No.' 'Westminster?' 'No.' 'Charing Cross?' 'Ah,' said the little girl in her tears, 'Yes, yes. Take me down to the cross and I can find my way home from there!'"

How true for all humanity, for all mankind, for our hopes and our hearts, and our lives! Take me to the cross and I can find my way home from there.

> I must needs go home
> By the way of the cross,
> There's no other way but this;
> I shall ne'er get sight
> Of the gates of light,
> If the way of the cross I miss.
>
> I must needs go on
> In the blood sprinkled way,
> The path that our Saviour trod,
> If I ever climb to the heights sublime,
> Where my soul is at rest with God.

This is God's invitation to you.

> What more can He say
> Than to you He hath said,
> To you who for refuge
> To Jesus have fled?

This is God's love and mercy poured out in the earth. This is God's sweet invitation to us today. Come, come.